Starting Right

Starting Right

A Basic Guide to Museum Planning

Gerald George

and

Cindy Sherrell-Leo

American Association for State and Local History
Nashville, Tennessee

Publication of this book was made possible in part by funds from the Charles Ulrick and Josephine Bay Foundation, Inc.

Designed by Gary Gore

Library of Congress Cataloguing-in-Publication Data

George, Gerald.
    Starting Right.
    Includes bibliographies and index.
    1. Museums—United States—Handbooks, manuals, etc.
I. Sherrell-Leo, Cindy. II. American Association for State and Local History. III. Title.
AM11.G46   1986   069'.0973   86-3400
ISBN 0-910050-78-3

Contents

Preface:
Getting a Museum Going

LET US GUESS who you are and what has brought you to this book.

You're a conscientious citizen who got mad when somebody threatened to tear down the handsome old passenger-train depot that had been a landmark in town for seventy years. You led a successful fight to save it. You promised to make it into a museum of art, science, or history.

OR: Your community is about to celebrate its centennial or bicentennial. The mayor has appointed you to a citizens' committee to establish a lasting commemorative for the occasion. You've recommended creating a museum to preserve your community's heritage.

OR: You're the president of your county's historical society. Someone has just given it a wonderful collection of wearing apparel from earlier times, or a huge file of historical photographs, or an attic full of antique furniture. There's just no room to display any of this in the historical society's office or library or meeting room. You realize that it's time for the society to expand into a museum.

OR: You chair the tourist-bureau committee at the Chamber of Commerce. On your recent vacation, you found yourself fascinated by another city's museum. You suppose that your city might attract more tourists if it, too, had a museum. You've persuaded the chamber to take the lead to get one started.

OR: You're an official with the Parks Department. It's just been given a historic site in your community, with some buildings on it. You're responsible for developing the site. You need a way to explain the site's significance to visitors. You plan to use one of the buildings for a visitor center with exhibits—a museum.

OR: You're a qualified archaeologist. You've just finished an interesting dig. You've turned up all kinds of Civil War relics or prehistoric artifacts. You want to develop a permanent public repository for them.

OR: You're on the board of an existing museum. Somebody has just willed it a private collection of paintings or old tools or stuffed animals. You'd like to expand your museum or create a new one to take care of the collection.

OR: You're a private collector with something special you'd like to give your community; but you want to be sure the community will keep your collection safe in perpetuity. You want to help the community create a museum that can preserve and use your collections.

Are any of those descriptions close?

If so, *this book is for you*. You're in a situation similar to that of hundreds of others who, every year—sometimes it seems every day—call our offices for advice on museum-making.

In fact, we've written this book because Americans are founding museums like never before. In 1910, America had only some 600 museums, but 2,500 were in operation by the outbreak of World War II. The 1986 *Official Museum Directory*, published by the American Association of Museums, lists 6,200 institutions. The American Association for State and Local History publishes a *Directory of Historical Agencies in North America*, which in 1986 had more than 13,000 entries, many of them museums or historical organizations that included museums. Counting all the kinds of museums—zoos, botanical gardens, aquariums, and art, science, and technology centers as well as museums of art, history, and natural history—we think the number of museums in operation today is approaching 10,000, if not already past that. Americans have been seized with museum mania. One goal of this book is to keep that pleasant state from becoming museum mayhem.

State and national organizations such as those where we work have helped scores of museum groups get going successfully. And in the process we've realized how much easier it would be if there were a how-to book available—just a little book, designed to explain in an evening's reading what somebody who is not a trained museum professional needs to know before starting a museum or expanding one. What does a museum need, to be successful? What are the right steps to take in order to achieve that? What are the kinds of costs, the legal responsibilities, the potential problems, the hidden pitfalls? We want to help you prepare for the proverbial alligators before you find yourself neck-deep in the swamp.

Part of the preparation is to let you know where to find more detailed sources of how-to-do-it information. There are many good books now available on museum work, along with other kinds of practical assistance. So, at the end of each chapter, we've included a short list of more technical reading matter that can be studied profitably on various aspects of museum operation.

Of course, you may already be a trained veteran of museum work who has been engaged to develop a new museum, or you may be a long-experienced trustee of a large, established museum that is creating a branch or extension. Even if you have a museum background and a major museum development in mind, the basic planning steps we identify in this book can be of use to you. Indeed, we hope this book will be valuable to anyone at the outset of any kind of museum planning.

Most museums in the United States are history museums, to one degree or another, and many began as community projects focusing on the heritage of the place where the museum founders live. Therefore, the advice and illustrations we offer in this book are presented primarily with community history museums in mind; but the principles that we identify apply to other kinds of museums as well.

The advice that we offer is far from original. It's a distillation of what we've learned from scores of museum professionals with whom we've had the privilege of working, one way or another, including unpaid volunteers who have applied professional skill to the operation of even the smallest museum. We owe gratitude to more persons than we ever could name in this short space, though we should like to crowd in a brief thanks at least to those who helped us with advice after reading the manuscript in draft: Kit Neumann and Curtis Tunnell of the Texas Historical Commission staff; Robert J. McQuarie, director of the Littleton Historical Museum; Betty Doak Elder and Patricia Hogan of the American Association for State and Local History staff; Jack Leo; Bob Sanders; and our editor, Martha Strayhorn.

And this book would not be available at all without grant assistance for its publication, for which we earnestly thank the Charles Ulrick and Josephine Bay Foundation, Inc., and its executive director Robert W. Ashton.

Overall, our purpose in putting this book together is to help the reader create a good museum plan. No book can make you a museum expert; that takes lots of study and experience. But we can provide basic guidance at the outset, including ways and places to find expertise, to keep your dream of a museum from turning into a nightmare. People like you who have taken time to look into museum requirements in advance have ultimately won the applause of their communities and have found museum development among the richest, most satisfying experiences of their lives.

We hope that will be the result for you.

Gerald George and Cindy Sherrell-Leo

Part I

What You Need to Know about It

The Old Dartmouth Historical Society in New Bedford, Massachusetts, invites children and adults to climb aboard the 89-foot scale model of the whaleship *Lagoda*, located in the Society's Whaling Museum. (Photograph courtesy of the Old Dartmouth Historical Society.)

1

Success Doesn't Equal Size

SO YOU WANT to start a museum?

Let's start at the end, rather than the beginning—let's see what your museum when ready might really look like. Let's do that by considering a couple of good, real museums that show what people like you and communities like yours actually can achieve. And let's relieve one of your anxieties right from the outset: Your museum is not going to have to be *huge* to be *good*. Unless your resources are extraordinary, you are not going to create a new Louvre or Smithsonian Institution—nothing on such a grand scale as that is required, or even necessarily desirable, for a museum to serve its community splendidly well.

For example. . . ?

Well, almost as far south as you can get in the state of Texas, just across the Rio Grande from Mexico, is a place that most visitors to the Louvre have never heard of: Hidalgo County, population (in the 1980 census) 283,229. Its county seat, Edinburg, had some 15,000 residents, fewer than the number of people who visit Smithsonian museums in a single week. But that small community, far from the more brilliant crowns of the museum world, developed one of its exquisite jewels.

The Hidalgo County Historical Museum opened its doors in April of 1970 after six years of careful planning and preparation. The work began in 1964, when a county survey committee prepared for a regional museum "in order that present and future generations will not only know the significance of the rich traditions of South Texas and Northern Mexico, but learn from the past," and recognize "the need to preserve this historical heritage which has been bestowed upon them." Theirs was a human heritage, stretching from Indian aboriginals and Spanish colonists through Mexican settlers and Anglo ranchers to the twentieth-century "Winter Texans" who flocked south temporarily each winter to escape the northern states' cold and snow.

The committee chose Edinburg for the museum site when the city made available an old jail built around 1910, of brick and white stucco with a red-tile roof, a windmill out back, and a "hanging tower" with a steel trapdoor inside. In 1967 the museum became incorporated as a nonprofit tax-exempt organization and began renovation of the jail in 1968. By the time of its opening, two years later, the museum had secured collections, planned exhibits, and hired a director to work with a group of volunteers.

From the start, the museum established, in writing, a clear, specific purpose: ". . . to maintain exhibits and collections pertaining to the history of the Rio Grande valley, the country and its people, with special emphasis on Hidalgo County. The rich heritage of this area is worthy of preservation. It is the obligation of this museum to assume the responsibilities of the collections which are held in trust for the benefit of the present and future citizens of the county."

Local accountants donated bookkeeping services and other citizens gave landscaping, artifacts, display cases, and mannequins, as well as historical artifacts and library materials. Volunteers washed windows, cleaned furniture, and addressed invitations. The museum opened five days a week and, in its first year, drew more than 2,800 visitors. Among the things they saw were temporary exhibits about each of the various towns in the county.

By 1985, fifteen years later, annual visitations had grown to more than 32,000. A new annex as well as the old jail contained imaginative exhibits on "the Indian Domain," Spanish exploration, border architecture, life on the "Old Ranches," and the way "Old Town" was around the turn of the twentieth century. The exhibits made use of old photos and maps in juxtaposition to early-day tools, household implements, ranching equipment, mercantile displays, clothing, weapons, and religious artifacts. The museum made itself, in its own words, "a place where you can touch time."

Moreover, depending on your age or special interests, you could do research in the museum's archives of material on the region's history, hear its regular lectures, take in its puppet shows and film series, or read its monthly newsletter and books it published on the region. Or if you were a school kid, a senior citizen in a nursing home, or the program director for a chamber of commerce or civic club, the museum would bring "outreach" programs to *you*.

At the museum itself, an elevator made exhibits accessible to handicapped visitors, and trained guides helped explain the artifacts, which by then totaled more than 15,000 items. New acquisitions were cleaned in accordance with basic rules of conservation, which included keeping artifacts away from fluorescent lights and direct sunlight and maintaining constant levels of temperature and relative humidity to prevent deterioration.

A board of eighteen citizens governed the museum, each serving a three-year term, with six trustees changing every year. They hired a staff, which by 1985 included five full-time employees: a curator of exhibits, a curator of collections, a building supervisor, and an administrative assistant, as well as the executive director. Also the museum had four part-time staff members and more than sixty active volunteers, who gave more than 7,000 hours of service annually and in-kind services worth $23,800.

The museum developed a Heritage Associates program to increase community involvement further and a Museum Guild to help raise money through such special events as an annual "Heritage Round-Up" festival. The county government provided 46 percent of the museum's budget, and the city of Edinburg another 9 percent. The rest came from individual contributions and earned income of various kinds, including sales in a small museum store.

At the close of its 1984 fiscal year, the museum reported income of $181,842 and expenditures of $165,872, which was impressive for a museum of its size, though of course far less than that of more famous ones. With a small endowment fund, total assets of more than a half-million dollars, and fund balances (in effect, net worth) of more than $400,000, the museum had a healthy balance sheet.

Moreover, throughout its development, the museum made use of other kinds of resources. Early on, it took advantage of on-site consultants available from and through the Museum and Field Services Department of the Texas Historical Commission, a state agency headquartered in Austin. Staff members of the museum attended short-term training programs, such as the periodic Winedale Seminars that the Texas Historical Commission provided on museum operations. Also staff members participated in meetings of professional associations, such as the Texas Association of Museums. Indeed, Executive Director Xenia F. T. (Fran) Alger served a term on the national Council of the American Association of Museums. And as this was written, the Hidalgo County Museum had applied to the American Association of Museums for accreditation, something only some six hundred museums in the country had achieved, including many gigantic ones.

Those six hundred accredited museums already included another museum that shows you don't have to be national in scope or gigantic in size to be excellent.

Out West, at the foot of the Rocky Mountains, lies Littleton, Colorado, a suburb of Denver. In the early 1980s, it had some 33,000 residents within the city limits, with a total of 120,000 within the greater Littleton area. They are the proud creators of the Littleton Historical Museum, accredited in 1978.

If you were a resident of that community in 1984, you would have received one day a green-and-white fold-out brochure with these words on the outside:

"Psst. . . what's the secret behind the trees on South Gallup St.?"

Inside, the brochure answered the question by describing the remarkable range of scenes that were part of Littleton's museum complex. First: a re-created turn-of-the-century farm, on which

> ". . . the whole family works from sunup to sundown. It seems the chores are never done. But an early spring planting and a good growing season could mean a bountiful harvest."

> Also—"a soot-darkened blacksmith shop. The bright glow from an open forge warms the shadowy interior. At the anvil, the blacksmith checks the temper of a newly sharpened plow blade, welds a broken wagon tire and puts his skills to work for the community."

> Next, Littleton's first schoolhouse, where—"soapstone pencils scrape and click against hard slate tablets, echoing sounds of lessons taught here more than 120 years ago."

> And then, an ice house—"using long saws and breaking bars, workers cut the first blocks of ice from a checker-board pattern scribed on the frozen lake. Men with long-handled picks guide the thick blocks up a

ramp into the ice house. The annual ice harvest has begun."

Yes, all of this, and finally the brochure described the main building, with offices and exhibit areas:

"Enter a special world. . . the museum is your doorway to discovery. Exhibits, programs, and demonstrations unlock the secrets of the past and future. Join us for the experience of another lifetime."

How did all of this come about?

The founders, long-time residents of Littleton, formed the Littleton Area Historical Society to hear speakers from time to time. Also they began collecting artifacts about the area's history, which they accumulated in a basement in the hope of developing exhibits some day. In the late 1960s, as the area grew in population, they particularly felt the need to inform all newcomers about the region's rich past.

At roughly the same time, the Littleton City Council got interested in developing a park on some land it had acquired. And next to that land was a beautiful private residence that a Littleton family decided it wished to sell. The family, the city, and the historical society linked up behind the museum idea. Members of the society raised money to buy the house, whose owners sold it at less than market value. The city then accepted the house as part of its new park, promising to establish and operate a museum in it and on the grounds, at public expense.

However, the founders sensibly went first to visit other museums in Colorado for advice. They also sought assistance from the Colorado Historical Society in Denver. There they particularly liked the help they got from a museum professional named Robert McQuarie, whom they enticed in the spring of 1969 to the position of paid staff director of their new organization. And in August of 1970, the Littleton Historical Museum officially opened, with a paid staff of four—the director, a curator of exhibits, a secretary, and a cabinet-maker/carpenter.

The stated purpose of the museum was to preserve and tell the history of the Littleton area in particular and its region in the West in general. The museum collected material from the beginnings of white settlement in the 1860s on up to the present time. In the first fifteen years of its own history, the museum amassed enough significant historical material to fill a 10,000-square-foot water tank, which it converted into a safe, secure, climate-controlled museum-storage facility.

The museum staff used those artifacts to present more than seventy different exhibits, ranging from a retrospective of works by an outstanding artist of the region to a presentation of the way people had to wash clothes before push-button machinery ended the drudgery of "Monday Blues."

In its first year, the museum operated with a budget of less than $20,000. By the early 1970s, it had become a full-fledged operating department of the city, under the city manager, just like the police and fire departments. In 1985 its budget had reached approximately $450,000, including support for ten full-time professionals plus five seasonal employees.

The city's own long-range planning included expansion of the museum itself in the 1970s and early 1980s beyond collecting and exhibiting in the museum-house. With fourteen contiguous acres available in the surrounding park, the museum also developed a living-history farm, a blacksmith shop, an ice house, and a school, to show what life was like for residents of the Littleton area when agriculture predominated in the period of 1895 to 1905.

That became the museum's carefully selected focal period, in part because the museum had good material with which to document and present that decade accurately. More recently, the museum began development of a second living-history farm, this one to show life in the region even earlier, in the 1860s and 1870s. The museum's staff also assumed responsibility to the city for preservation of historic buildings generally. The museum itself acquired two old railroad depots, one of which it adapted for use as a fine-arts gallery for the community.

The museum also became a regular resource for the city's schools, providing them programs continuously throughout the school year and offering a summer-education program called "Experiences in History." It provided ten week-long "workshops" at the museum's historic facilities, a chance for children "to experience the joys and disappointments of a lifestyle of the past." Each day, pupils from the second through the sixth grades came on site to assume the roles of nineteenth-century adults and learn from the museum staff to "become printers, carpenters, farmers, blacksmiths, weavers—all builders of a community."

Some five hundred families in Littleton helped support special projects at the museum through a membership organization called "Friends of the Library and Museum." But the museum did not charge admission or promote itself as a tourist attraction to make money. Of its visitors, 90 percent were local or area residents, payers of the taxes that supported the museum, which consciously strove to provide educational experiences of particular interest to them.

The Littleton Museum does not operate in isolation, however, any more than does the Hidalgo County Historical Museum. Director McQuarie is a former member of the governing councils of both the American Association of Museums and the American Association for State and Local History. He and members of his staff have participated also in the Colorado-Wyoming Museums Association, the Mountain-Plains Museums Association, and related service groups.

The Natural History Museum of Los Angeles County and New

York's Metropolitan Museum of Art are bigger in budget and staff, but that doesn't keep the Littletons or the Hidalgo counties of America from having splendid museums. You and your community can, too, if you'll plan as carefully and conscientiously as they did for what it takes.

And—if you know what a museum really is. . . !

For more information

To find established museums of sizes and types similar to what you have in mind, consult the *Official Museum Directory,* published by the American Association of Museums and the National Register Publishing Company, 3004 Glenview Road, Wilmette, Illinois 60091; and the *Directory of Historical and Agencies in North America,* published by the the American Association for State and Local History, 172 Second Avenue, North, Suite 102, Nashville, Tennessee 37201.

Your own state's museum association or historical society, likely to be located in your state's capital city, may have lists of museums that are relatively close to you.

Descriptions of small museums that have become accredited are available from the American Association of Museums, P.O. Box 33399, Washington, D.C. 20033, in a 27-page, illustrated pamphlet entitled *Small Museums and Accreditation.*

Reports on the achievements of state and local history museums appear regularly in *History News,* the magazine of the American Association for State and Local History (see address above).

Also there is much descriptive material on the range and concerns of American museums today in *Museums for a New Century,* a report of the Comission on Museums for a New Century, published in 1984 by the American Assoication of Museums, Washington, D.C. It is illustrated, with an index and appendices, in 144 pages.

A Culture at Risk: Who Cares for America's Heritage? (95 pages), by Charles Phillips and Patricia Hogan, published by AASLH Press in 1984, offers a profile—past and present—of the nation's historical agencies, many of which are museums.

2

History Is Right behind You

AND WHAT really is a museum?

Let's not worry yet about trying to define museums in the abstract. Instead, let's see who some more of your predecessors were and what they thought they were doing. After all, Hidalgo County, Texas, and Littleton, Colorado, did not begin the museum movement. There is a long tradition of museum experience behind us, and we can learn something from museum history. We can learn how the museums of recent time began and what they have *become*.

More than two centuries ago, Sir Hans Sloane wanted to start a museum. He was a distinguished English doctor who became physician-general of the British army and president of the Royal College of Physicians. He also was a traveler and a collector in an age when science was on the rise and curious people throughout Europe were assembling collections of all kinds of things to study.

Sir Hans himself had two hundred large volumes of dried samples of plants from all over the world, more than five thousand insect specimens, tons of shells and stones, including human kidney and bladder stones, and much more from nature's great variety. His inventory included "eggs" and "vipers" and "fishes and their parts" and "quadrupeds and their parts."

But also, he had vast collections of things made by humans—ancient urns, instruments, and other products of antiquity, plus

23

many books, manuscripts, and pictorial materials. He had thirty-two thousand medals and coins.

In scope, his collection was not unlike something that many American communities have had on a smaller scale—the kind of "museum" you may have visited as a school kid, where you saw cases full of stuffed animals next to cabinets of rocks and minerals and birds' nests and sea shells, in the same room with collections of Lincoln-head pennies and Indian arrowheads neatly mounted for display on the walls.

But neither that nor Sir Hans's huge collection was yet, in the modern sense, a museum.

What Sir Hans possessed used to be called a "cabinet of curiosities," and he kept it for the private edification of himself and selected scientists and for the amazement or amusement of other friends. Then one day in 1753, fifty of those friends— or at least fifty prominent Englishmen—woke up to discover that Sir Hans wanted them to organize something different.

Each of the fifty received word that Sir Hans had died, that in his will he had named them all as trustees of his collection, and that he had charged them to keep all he had collected together by selling it to the king of England, or—failing that— to some scholarly organization such as the Royal Society or Oxford University or to the king of some other country.

Why? In order that the things he had collected would, as he said, "remain together, and not be separated, and that chiefly in and about the City of London. . . where they may by the great confluence of people be of most use," under the care of some public body for the "benefit of mankind."

Yes—the benefit of mankind.

If you have visited London, you may have seen something from Sir Hans's collection—for it, and two other collections that the king and the Parliament eventually assented to buy, constitute the beginning of the famed British Museum, which is visited every year by thousands of scholars and ordinary citizens of countries throughout the world.

An *organization* to take *permanent care* of *significant objects* for the *public good*—the basic elements of a modern museum thus came together. Not just a building, not just a collection, and certainly not just for fun.

The British Museum was not the only such organization in earlier times, or even necessarily the first one. And as museums developed, there were lots of different notions by lots of different founders about what their organizations would contribute to the public good.

Nearly forty years after the death of Sir Hans, in Revolutionary France in the 1790s, the Republicans who took over the Royal Palace at Versailles stood amazed when they found themselves the possessors of the king's magnificent collection of works of art. Should these treasures be destroyed as symbols of the opulence of the oppressive old regime? No, they decided instead to claim these works for the common people and put them nearer the people in the former royal palace in Paris for democratic enlightenment and inspiration.

Thus was created what we know today as the Louvre, one of the more famous of the world's art museums, which annually attracts thousands of tourists to see the smile of the Mona Lisa, among other artistic treasures of many ages. Napoleon enriched the Louvre's collection with works of art plundered from the foreign countries he conquered as the French Revolution extended into empire.

Directing the Louvre for Napoleon was one Dominique Vivant Denon, an art collector who himself often appeared on fields of battle, even before the bullets had stopped flying. He and Napoleon intended their museum to demonstrate the glory of France. And Denon distinguished himself not only by his taste in what he selected for the Louvre, but also by the ingenuity with which he made it a museum for public use. Arranging the paintings in a logical, understandable order, improving the internal lighting, and even arguing for the installation of public restrooms, Denon worked to entice the public to visit. Indeed, one could make a case that museum development has been part of the democratization of culture that characterizes the last few centuries almost everywhere.

Certainly something like that was in the mind of Sir Henry Cole, another English innovator. In 1851, well after Napoleon's demise, Cole was the guiding genius behind London's Great Exhibition of the Industry of All Nations, held in the Crystal Palace. When the exhibition closed, after visits by six million people, Sir Henry and its royal patrons, Prince Albert and Queen Victoria, wanted to continue its purpose—to "extend the influence of science and art upon productive industry." The eventual result was the South Kensington Museum, which became the greatest museum of the decorative arts in the world. But Sir Henry saw it also as an instrument of social reform, and he even kept it open at night, so that the masses could come to it after work, instead of "to the gin palace."

There were at least two other famous museum developments in the nineteenth and early twentieth centuries in Europe. Artur Hazelius in Sweden opened Skansen, a folk museum that included an outdoor section with costumed guides and craft demonstrations to show the life styles of earlier times. He wished to keep national traditions alive in the face of rapid industrial growth and technological change. Technology itself became the subject of the Deutsches Museum that Oskar von Miller developed in Germany. He was a civil engineer who organized electrical exhibitions to demonstrate the possibilities of long-distance power transmission. And he wanted a museum that would help young people in particular to understand new technology by seeing devices in action and even touching them.

But all the good ideas in public-purpose museum development didn't come out of Europe. On our side of the Atlantic, not long before the Louvre became an art museum, an itinerant, ill-educated portrait painter named Charles Willson Peale was on his way from Maryland to Philadelphia. There, he established a museum by assembling an Allegheny River paddlefish, the skeleton of a mastodon, a bunch of mounted birds in realistic poses in front of painted backgrounds, and some portraits of the Founding Fathers of the United States. He charged admission, and the techniques of exhibition and interpretation that he pioneered to make education in the museum a pleasure have influenced museum directors ever since.

Also there was Ann Pamela Cunningham, whose work has so greatly influenced America's historic-house museums. The story goes that, in the middle of the last century, this frail young woman received a letter from her mother describing the sad ruin of the Virginia home of George Washington. ". . . And the thought passed through my mind, " her mother wrote, "why was it that the women of his country did not try to keep it in repair if the men could not do it. It does seem such a blot on our country."

The younger Ms. Cunningham agreed and, indeed, gave her life to that cause. She founded the Mount Vernon Ladies' Association of the Union, which saved the property and made it a historic-house museum to inspire public patriotism. But part of her influence came from her success in fighting off extravagant schemes for transforming Mount Vernon into a shrine at the expense of accurate historical restoration. She wrote: "Those who go to the home in which [George Washington] lived and died, wish to see in what he lived and died. Let one spot in this grand country of ours be saved from 'change'!"

And what of the Smithsonian Institution? Its huge museums

line the mall in downtown Washington, D.C., where busloads of us make pilgrimages to see exhibits of art, history, anthropology, natural history, technology, and much else. A museum innovator named George Brown Goode had much to do with their development. In 1879 he took charge of what was then known as the Smithsonian's "national museum," which he wanted to make "a nursery of living thoughts" rather than "a cemetery of bric-a-brac." His legacy is in these words: "The museum of the future must stand side by side with the library and the laboratory, as part of the teaching equipment of the college and university, and in the great cities co-operate with the public library as one of the principal agencies for the enlightenment of the people."

Does such public enlightenment depend on such comprehensive collections of spectacular things as the Smithsonian now has—Rembrandts and elephants, locomotives and spaceships and jewels? Certainly not, was the answer of another museum founder, whose museum-education ideas any community or group could adopt.

This was John Cotton Dana, a librarian by training who in 1909 found himself in charge of the new Newark Museum in New Jersey. An argumentative man who delighted in shocking other directors of museums by declaring that nobody really knew how to run one, Dana sought ways to make education enjoyable "for the mechanic, clerk and salesman" as well as "the professional man and man of leisure." He also encouraged women to visit his museum and trained women to work in it. He was not too proud to use advertising to entice visitors, nor averse to adapting new technology to serve its purposes, such as machines that could pose and answer questions.

He contended that "a good museum attracts, entertains, arouses curiosity, leads to questioning—and thus promotes learning. To do these things a museum can use simple, common, and inexpensive objects. . . to awaken young and old to interest and inquiry about the world outside themselves."

What we've now given you is hardly a comprehensive history of museum development. But it is enough to convey an idea, transcending some dry definition, of what a good museum can be—a public entry-way to worlds outside ourselves, worlds created by nature and humankind, worlds discovered by scientists, imagined by artists, transformed by technological innovators, and worlds lived in by earlier generations whose ways of life were different from our own.

Museums go back to ancient Egypt and Japan. Our word *museum* itself comes from classical Greece and Rome. Medieval churches preserved works of art and religious relics. Renaissance humanists displayed collections in cabinets and galleries. University museums developed in Basel, Switzerland, and Oxford, England, well before Sir Hans Sloane and others helped make museums into public institutions. In the New World, museums date back at least to the 1770s. But most American museums began in our own century. By the 1980s, they ranged from the Metropolitan Museum of Art in New York City to California's San Diego Zoo, a museum exhibiting live specimens; from Colonial Williamsburg, which has restored for exhibition an entire eighteenth-century Virginia town, to the U.S.S. *Arizona* Memorial in Pearl Harbor, Hawaii; from the Alaska State Museum, with its exhibits of native American artifacts in Juneau, to the Children's Museum of Oak Ridge in Tennessee.

In between are the Living History Farms near Des Moines, Iowa; the tiny Tintic Mining Museum in central Utah; Shakertown at Pleasant Hill, Kentucky, where a southeastern community of the Shaker religious sect once lived; the Afro-American Historical and Cultural Museum in Philadelphia; and the Civil War battlefield museums of the National Park Service. Also there are now big state museums in Oregon and Kansas, Tennessee, and Maine. There are such regional museums as the Panhandle-Plains Historical Museum in Canyon, Texas, and the Historical Museum of Southern Florida in Miami. And there are hundreds of city and town and county museums, which, as George Brown Goode advocated, are taking their places beside colleges and schools and public libraries as cultural centers for their communities.

Some of today's "museums" are still just cabinets of curiosities or the playthings of self-designated elite groups. But many are real museums. If that's truly what you want, then some early questions you must answer are:

Can you organize—
      —to collect significant things?
      —to care for them perpetually?
      —and to use them for public good?

And by entering the museum universe, can you, too, awaken your fellow humans to worlds outside themselves?

For more information

On the history and nature of museums, we strongly recommend two excellent books on which we have relied for much of the information in this chapter. Both are by Dr. Edward P. Alexander, former director of the Museum Studies Program at the University of Delaware, and throughout his career a leader in the museum field. The books are *Museums in Motion: An Introduction to the History and Functions of Museums* (308 pages), illustrated, with an index and bibliography, published in 1979 by the American Association for State and Local History, Nashville, Tennessee; and *Museum Masters: Their Museums and Their Influence* (428 pages), illustrated, with an index and bibliographies, also published by the American Association for State and Local History in 1983.

On the history of historic-house and historic site museums, the reader might also wish at least to sample the detailed volumes of Charles B. Hosmer, Jr.: *Presence of the Past: A History of the Preservation Movement in the United States Before Williamsburg* (New York: G. P. Putnam's Sons, 1965), and *Preservation Comes of Age: From Williamsburg to the National Trust,* 2 vols. (Charlottesville: University Press of Virginia, 1981.)

A large, brown bear greets visitors at the University of Alaska Museum in Fairbanks. (Photograph courtesy of the University of Alaska Museum, Fairbanks.)

3

Respect Is the Overall Rule

NOW YOU KNOW what museums have become and that towns and counties, as well as states and cities, can have good ones. But what, exactly, makes a museum good?

The term *museum* has come to embrace zoos, botanical gardens, science and technology centers, public art galleries, and historic houses, as well as traditional museums of art, anthropology, archaeology, history, and natural history. But they all have one thing in common—they put us in contact with *real things*, an original Picasso painting, a genuine precious gem, a stuffed elephant, a living tortoise, the bones of a prehistoric monster, a Civil War sword, a furnished Victorian house, a spinning wheel in operation, the eye of a fly seen under magnification, a functioning engine rigged up for demonstration, the desk where Lincoln signed the Emancipation Proclamation, or even a display of the original document itself. *And there really is only one principle of museum organization and operation—respect for the "real thing."* One could almost define a museum as an organization for evaluating things, or imputing significance to them. Certainly a good museum is one in which respect for its real things underlies everything it does.

What exactly does that mean?

Let us try to illustrate with a simple example. Let us take you on an imaginary visit to see a rather standard and uncomplicated kind of museum exhibit. To break down the old notion that a museum is necessarily a building, let us envision this imaginary exhibit housed in a "history van" that has just arrived in your community, on tour from your state's historical society. And let us assume that the exhibit in the van commemorates the anniversary of a battle of major importance that took place near your community.

As you enter, the first thing you see in the exhibit is the actual flag that your predecessors in the community carried into that battle. You learn about that from reading the signs (or *labels,* as museum people call them) on the glass-enclosed case in which the old flag is displayed, unfurled. Or you hear about it from a guide (or *docent,* as museum people say) who takes groups through the exhibit. Or you learn it from listening to the tape in the electronic guide that you rented or borrowed when you came in.

From one of those sources you also learn that the flag was handmade, that its design was devised by the military group that carried it into battle, that only one or two others of the same design from the same period still exist, and that at a crucial moment in the battle somebody rallied the eventually victorious side by courageously hoisting this flag once more after its wounded bearer had momentarily let it fall. The significance of that old piece of fabric on a pole strikes home as you see, behind it in the case, an enlarged eye-witness sketch or an old photo of the battlefield with that same flag being raised above it. And in the rest of the exhibit you learn what differences that battle made—what happened to your community, your region, your state or country in consequence of that victory—how the course of history changed, in this place, because of the outcome of that battle.

Now—just think about it. Somebody obviously has gone to a lot of trouble to make the sight of that old flag a significant experience for you. Someone wanted to share with you an appreciation of a historical object—its beauty, originality, and impressive craftsmanship. Someone wanted to invoke the educational potential of that object—its ability to arouse your interest, to capture your imagination, to make real to you a human event of significance. Somebody, in fact, wanted to impress you with the sheer power of that object—the dramatic realization that the battle fought here wasn't just a story in a book, but was a real cataclysmic struggle by real, sweating, shouting people, who a century or more ago created and carried and were inspired by this object, this flag, the very same that you are seeing now.

Clearly, somebody within the museum has profound respect for that old flag. Respect enough to do extensive research to document its authenticity and explain its significance. Respect enough to make labels and tapes or train docents to make information about it available to you. Respect enough to arrange the flag in a case so you can study it. Respect enough even to haul it to your community in a van, for you to visit conveniently.

Research and interpretation, museum people call such preparatory work with historical objects. And research and interpretation are activities that good museums perform.

Some museum people respect their objects so much that they try to make them accessible to every imaginable group of viewers. In our imaginary van, they put up a ramp for people who can't climb steps or for viewers confined to wheelchairs. They provide short, simple labels at eye-level for school-age children, as well as longer, fuller labels, higher up, for adults. And if your area has a sizeable population of speakers of Spanish—or some other language besides English—the labels and docent-spiels may be bilingual.

But research, interpretation, and accessible exhibition are not the only signs of respect for a museum's "real things." No, there is a great deal more.

If you think about it, the other things required if one respects objects will be clear. For one thing, respect for an object obviously includes keeping track of it. Consider our imaginary exhibit again. That wonderful old flag did not leave its storage area without authorization by the appropriate museum official, who recorded when and where it went, what condition it was in, and when it would be back. In fact, when the museum first got the flag, someone with registration responsibilities set up a record file on it, manually or in a computer. There one can find out when and from whom the flag was received, what condition it arrived in, whether it came as a gift or a loan—and if a loan, for how long—and what is known about it.

Such records help the museum keep track of its holdings and protect them from loss and also help make the objects accessible for use. A year from now, someone may want to send out the history van again, not with the battle exhibit, but with a full exhibit of military flags themselves—the different kinds that military units have adopted, with information on what they were made of, how they were used, what alterations in construction and use of the banners took place as changes occurred in the technology and organization of warfare itself. A search of the files for military flags for such an exhibit will turn up our flag, as well as others, if the records are properly and carefully kept. Or suppose a military historian is studying flags in museum collections as part of the research needed for a book on that subject. Research as well as exhibit development depends on good museum records, including keeping track of where objects are and what condition they are in.

That's another thing, of course: Respect for an object requires caring about its condition. Our flag will not be available for exhibition or research very long if it gets stolen from the van or damaged while in it. So, precautions are taken to protect it. There are no windows in the van—or, if there is a window, the flag is not put in front of it, because direct sunlight harms textiles. The van is protected against insects such as moths. And throughout the van—or at least in the area where the flag is displayed—temperature and relative humidity are controlled to prevent damaging fluctuations and excessive levels of both. Placement in the glass case protects the flag also from vandalism, as does the security system for the van itself, which may include television monitors and electronic sensing devices, as well as locks and keys.

Earlier, when the museum people mounted the flag in its case, they took care not to use nails or tacks that might snag the cloth and tear it. They constructed special fabric backings fixed to panels that enable textiles to be displayed with minimal strain on their fabrics. *Conservation* is what museum people call all of these protective measures. Some museum staffs include highly trained conservators.

In fact, if the flag truly is respected, it will be kept in a protected, secure, climate-controlled storage area when it isn't in the van or elsewhere on exhibit or being studied by someone. And before it is put into the van, someone checks it to see if it has remained sturdy enough to withstand travel. When it is returned to the home museum, it will be checked again, just as it was when first received, to see whether it needs cleaning or repair or treatment to prevent further deterioration, all using methods that conservators judge safe for fragile textiles. For ours, you see, is a chemically unstable planet, where everything is more or less subject to deterioration all the time. Respect for museum objects—"real things"—requires prolonging their useful life as long as possible.

Research, interpretation, exhibition, registration, conservation, and security—even this is not a complete list of what respect for museum collections requires. For even with all these things, the flag could still wind up in the city dump when the van returns if, in the interim, the museum has gone broke, or its staff lacks facilities or training, or its board of trustees fails to plan ahead. Respect also requires fund-raising, long-range planning, and development of both staff and facilities so that objects in the collections can be cared for adequately and used effectively. Nothing is sadder than seeing an old battle flag survive war only to be destroyed by careless museum administration.

And museum administration is more difficult in many ways than regular profit-making business administration. Inventory reduction, for one instance, is not a problem for businesses; it may be a sign of sales success. But a museum *collects and keeps,* more or less forever. The respect we have for the historic battle flag is different from the respect we have, for say, the typewriter on which this book is written. We take care of the typewriter, hoping that it will serve us for several years. If it lasts so long as to become rare and enters a museum's collections, the museum will need to maintain it not only for the present but for future generations. A good museum not only treats its objects with respect *now;* it agrees to do so in perpetuity.

Because some valuable "real things" are extremely fragile, museums exhibit them only rarely, or make them accessible only for qualified research. Some museums use reproductions in exhibits and interpretive programs. Some collect multiple examples of the same object, so that, when one wears out, others will be available. Some museums don't maintain collections of their own at all, but provide opportunities for viewing traveling exhibits, or draw upon collections of others to assemble new exhibits. Museums of the future may rely less on exhibits and more on electronic devices, video, and laser technology, to convey a sense of "real things." And the amount of research, interpretation, conservation, and so on that we give an object varies, depending on what we respect it *for.* The kind of descriptive label used to explain the historical significance of photographs of nineteenth-century businessmen in our town, for example, might seem to get in the way of the aesthetic experience we seek from unimpeded gazing at Whistler's painting of his mother, about whom biographical information would seem less relevant. Moreover, there are many ways to "read" an artifact, varying from the way it was made and used to the psychological meaning and value it may have had.

Nonetheless, the very act of seeking or accepting an object for a museum collection imputes significance to it. A natural specimen, a work of art, a historical artifact—each has some special value, even if only as an educational tool, or we would not keep it in preference to hundreds of other objects. Research may enhance our respect for some object, or changing tastes diminish it. But museums are in the business of assessing the significance of tangible things, and all the different aspects of museum work are, in essence, logical extensions of respect for the things we decide are worth keeping.

The principle of respect has been codified in a basic guide to responsible museum work—the accreditation standards of the American Association of Museums. To be accredited, a museum must be "an organized and permanent nonprofit institution, essentially educational or aesthetic in purpose, with professional staff, which owns and utilizes tangible objects, cares for them and exhibits them to the public on some regular schedule."

On-site teams that evaluate museums for accreditation use checklists that include 171 specific questions about governing authority, boards of trustees, staff, membership, finances, physical facilities, collections, conservation, security, exhibits, educational programs, purposes, and future plans. The standards are sometimes debated and subject to change, but not the basic notion that much is required to show real respect for such museum objects as that old battle flag. The goal is: *Long may it wave!*

For more information

The museum accreditation standards mentioned in this chapter are found in an 80-page paperback booklet entitled *Professional Standards for Museum Accreditation: The Handbook of the Accreditation Program of the American Association of Museums,* edited by H. J. Swinney and published in 1978 by the American Association of Museums in Washington, D.C.

For more information on the range of museum responsibilities and activities, we recommend two basic texts that non-professionals will find helpful:

Introduction to Museum Work, by G. Ellis Burcaw, 2nd edition, 1983 (209 pages), illustrated and indexed, with recommended resources, published by the American Association for State and Local History, Nashville, Tennessee.

The Management of Small History Museums, by Carl E. Guthe, 2nd edition, 1964 (80 pages), published also by AASLH.

For readers who do decide to go ahead with museum creation, we also recommend two slightly more detailed works whose contents cover all major aspects of museum work:

Planning Our Museums, edited by Barry Lord and Gail Dexter Lord, a 309-page looseleaf notebook published in 1983 by the National Museums of Canada and distributed in the United States by AASLH.

Manual for Museums, by Ralph H. Lewis, 1976 (408 pages), published by the National Park Service, Washington, D.C.

4

Help Is All about You

THE IDEA you now have of all the things it takes to make a good museum may seem a little overwhelming. Like a swimmer suddenly in deep water with a strong tide, you may feel like yelling "Help!" At least it should by now be evident that a museum demands expertise and experience and time, just as your business or profession does. You didn't learn banking or farming or the law or school-teaching or librarianship overnight, and museum work can be equally complicated and demanding. But experience and expertise is available to you, if you know how to find and use it.

Let's assume that it's the morning after your community made the decision to start a new museum and appointed you to chair the committee to do it. Why you? Probably because you started a successful car dealership from scratch and also everybody knows you're a Civil War buff. Or maybe you majored in art history in college, and you've been the prime mover and workhorse behind other cultural activities in your city. Or possibly you've retired after a distinguished military career and have some time on your hands—a former army officer ought to be able to handle anything, right?

Your clear head and ability to solve problems are likely the qualities that made your peers select you to spearhead the new museum. You'll put those qualities to immediate use. The first thing you'll do, on your first morning as museum-committee chair, is call up your state's historical society or historical commission, or your state's museum association, or your state's state museum. Almost every state has one or the other, and in almost every state such organizations are found in the state's capital city.

The first question you ask is this: What laws and regulations pertain to museum organizations in your state? It's a good idea to have a local lawyer already on your committee, especially if he or she is willing to contribute *pro bono publico* some research on nonprofit incorporation, tax-exemption application, and legal responsibilities of public-trust institutions such as museums. But the state agency you call may be able to put that information into your hands without research, or at least identify for you the relevant sections of your state's legal code. States do have laws that pertain to museums, and museums have in fact been sued for not paying attention to them.

Next you should ask whether the state agency you are calling, or any other known to it, has a field-service or museum-consultant program. If you are lucky, you live in a state that respects its heritage enough to support a field-services staff, which can help museums, historical societies, county historical commissions, or historic-preservation organizations. Texas, for example, has both the Texas Association of Museums, a professionally staffed, membership-supported state museum association, and the Texas Historical Commission, a tax-supported state historical agency. The latter has a Museum and Field Services Department that has been putting two to three staff members almost continuously on the road to consult directly with museums and other heritage organizations statewide, including new ones. States such as Iowa, Minnesota, Ohio, and Wisconsin have had strong local-history programs which operate out of their state historical societies and provide advice at least to historical museums. Some state museums have housed traveling "museum coordinators," or regularly shared experts from their in-house staffs, such as the conservator whom the Tennessee State Museum has made available to help others statewide.

If you can't get an experienced museum person to come out to meet with you, you might next ask whether a professional in one of the state agencies would be willing to let you and others on your committee come there to meet for advice. Or someone in a state agency may be able to recommend a private museum consultant, if you can afford to hire outside expertise. Some dependable professional consultants are available, though it's wise to check credentials with previous clients and other museum professionals or organizations. Also, experienced museum people sometimes are willing to moonlight from their regular jobs by accepting an occasional paid consultantship.

The next question to ask over the phone is where to get a descriptive list of museums already established in your state, so that you can determine which ones might be best for you and your committee to visit, in light of the kind and size of museum you have in mind. Your state museum association almost certainly will have a directory of museums in the state and should be able to lead you to the best examples of comparable museums.

Trying to arrange behind-the-scenes visits to established museums of the kind you want to create is almost essential for the development of realistic plans, and you may want to extend your search for good models beyond your state's borders to your region or even nationally. Regional and national museum associations also publish directories, often organized by state, and can advise you by phone or mail about good museums to visit for your purposes. National and regional museum-service organizations are listed at the end of this chapter.

The question to ask last, if at all, is where to get money for developing your museum. Later chapters will deal more extensively with that, but as a general rule, neither government agencies nor private museum associations at the national, regional, or state levels have grants or other financial assistance for new museums. *If you can't count on local government or private support in your own community to get a museum going, public interest may not be high enough to make the effort worthwhile.* At this point, if your spadework is bringing to light great indifference or—worse—apathy, it is wise to consider, before going further, the fact that until a community *wants* a museum enough to support one, it really may not need one.

Once you finish the phone calls to find out about state laws, get advice from state agencies or state associations, arrange for consultants, and identify appropriate places for site visits, the time will have come to begin exploring sources you can tap for help that your museum will need as it moves along. The first day of your effort is not too soon to write to all relevant regional and national museum-service organizations for information on everything they offer.

The American Association of Museums (AAM), for example, represents museums of all kinds, including zoos and planetariums and botanical gardens. Started in 1906 as a nonprofit organization, the AAM has both institutional and individual members, some of whom also belong to its standing committees, which include the Trustees Committee and the Small Museums Committee. AAM publishes a magazine, *Museum News*, and a newsletter, *Aviso,* along with books and reports of use to the museum field. Also its legislative program represents the interests of museums in Washington, D.C., seeing that the needs of museums are understood by the Congress, by federal agencies that make grants or administer tax policy, and by others. In addition to the AAM Accreditation Program that we mentioned earlier, AAM developed in the early 1980s a Museum Assessment Program (MAP), through which *established* museums can get on-site consultants to help them evaluate their needs, strengths, and weaknesses prior to, or independently of, applying for accreditation. This won't help you at the outset, but if the Institute of Museum Services, a tax-supported federal agency, continues to fund MAP, it can eventually be of great help in your museum's development.

The American Association for State and Local History (AASLH) is another major source of help for museums. AASLH began in 1940 as a nonprofit association with both individual and institutional members. Though most AASLH members work with history, particularly in historical societies, historic sites, archives, and historic houses as well as museums, AASLH publications have been useful to a great range of museums. AASLH publishes a magazine, *History News,* and a newsletter, *History News Dispatch,* along with regular Technical Reports on special topics in museum and historical agency work from the AASLH Technical Information Service. The AASLH Press offers a catalogue of how-to-do-it books on almost every phase of museum work, and AASLH has for several years offered seminars, workshops, audiovisual training kits, independent-study courses, and a consultant service for established museums.

Other national nonprofit membership associations also provide valuable help to art museums, science museums, and many other kinds. So do the six regional museum associations that cover the United States. In Canada, the Canadian Museums Association and the provincial museum associations offer many kinds of help.

Whether you remain a trustee of your museum or whether, at least at the outset, you undertake some day-to-day responsibility or more direct administrative role, you and your co-workers can use the museum associations at all levels to develop your expertise. In addition to helpful publications, the state, regional, and national associations all have annual meetings, which typically include sessions for people who need basic how-to-do-it information, as well as help at intermediate and advanced levels. All such meetings will give you the opportunity to compare notes with others and seek solutions to common problems. Additionally, special seminars and workshops are likely to be available near you from your state historical society or museum association, your regional museum association, or one of the national museum-service groups. Subjects typically include how to improve fund-raising and public relations, how to give your collections basic care, and how to make effective exhibits.

Then—lo and behold, who knows?—if you yourself get hooked on museum work, you may decide to turn the car dealership over to Junior, or give up your volunteer cultural activities, or abandon golf as an insufficiently challenging occupation for a former military leader, and pursue a whole new career. Then you'll want to think about short-term training programs for overall development of museum skills, such as the ten-day Winedale Seminar on museum administration that the Texas Historical Commission periodically has offered, or the four-week Seminar for Historical Administration at Colonial Williamsburg, which has been co-sponsored annually for many years by AASLH, AAM, Colonial Williamsburg, and the National Trust for Historic Preservation, or the Museum Management Institute, sponsored by the Getty Trust, the Art Museum Association of America, and the University of California, Berkeley.

In the 1970s and 1980s, many universities have developed formal degree programs for people who wish to pursue careers in museums. AASLH, AAM, and other associations can guide you to lists of such programs, as well as to standards for evaluating them. It is useful to know about such programs, even if you yourself will do no more than judge the credentials of museum professionals whom you may want to hire. But universities also are increasingly becoming sources of publications, regional conferences, and special programs of help in museum work generally. You might check for such programs at the university nearest you.

Well—now you have a good idea of what you may be getting into. The field you are thinking of entering has a long and exciting history of creative development. You don't have to have a big museum or extraordinary collections to "do good" in it. You do have to respect your collections in every way, from the use you make of them to the care you provide for them. And there is a great network of state, provincial, regional, and national organizations to help you do it. But before you finally say, "Okay, let's give it a shot and go ahead," the next chapter tells you one more thing you need to know, namely— *you don't have to do it!*

For more information

Depending on what kind of museum you are starting, one or more of the following organizations can help if you write for information on their publications, programs, and services. Addresses are as reported in the 1986 edition of *The Official Museum Directory;* please check for changes in later editions as they appear.

I. National Organizations

African-American Museums Association
420 Seventh Street, N.W.
Washington, D.C. 20004

American Arts Alliance
424 C Street, N.E.
Washington, D.C. 20002

American Association for State and Local History
172 Second Avenue, North, Suite 102
Nashville, Tennessee 37201

American Association of Botanical Gardens & Arboreta
Department of Horticulture
Box 3530
Las Cruces, New Mexico 88003

American Association of Museums
1055 Thomas Jefferson Street, N.W.
Washington, D.C. 20007

American Association of Youth Museums
Lutz Children's Museum
247 Main Street
Manchester, Connecticut 06040

American Association of Zoological Parks & Aquariums
Oglebay Park
Wheeling, West Virginia 26003

American Institute for Conservation
of Historic and Artistic Works (AIC)
3545 Williamsburg Lane, N.W.
Washington, D.C. 20008

Art Museum Association
270 Sutter Street
San Francisco, California 94108

Association for Living Historical Farms
and Agricultural Museums
National Museum of American History
Washington, D.C. 20560

Association of Art Museum Directors
1130 Sherbrook Street, West
Montreal, Quebec H3A 2R5 CANADA

Association of Railroad Museums, Inc.
33 Ashland Street
Manchester, New Hampshire 03104

Association of Science Museum Directors
Field Museum of Natural History
Roosevelt Road and Lake Shore Drive
Chicago, Illinois 60605

Association of Science-Technology Centers
1413 K Street, N.W.
Washington, D.C. 20005

Association of Systematics Collections
Museum of Natural History
University of Kansas
Lawrence, Kansas 66045

Association of Volunteer Committees
of Museums of Canada and the United States
P.O. Box 774, Station B
Ottawa, Ontario K1P 5A0 CANADA

Canadian Museums Association
280 rue Metcalfe Street, Suite 202
Ottawa, Ontario K2P 1R7 CANADA

Council of American Maritime Museums
Maritime Museum
P.O. Box 636
St. Michaels, Maryland 21663

Council for Museum Anthropology
Lowie Museum of Anthropology
University of California
Berkeley, California 94720

Museum Reference Center
A & I Building, Room 2235
Smithsonian Institution
Washington, D.C. 20560

Museum Store Association
61 S. Pine Street
Doylestown, Pennsylvania 18901

National Institute for the Conservation
of Cultural Property
A & I Building, Room 2225
Smithsonian Institution
Washington, D.C. 20560

National Trust for Historic Preservation
1785 Massachusetts Avenue, N.W.
Washington, D.C. 20036

North American Indian Museums Association
Seneca-Iroquois National Museum
P.O. Box 442
Salamanca, New York 14779

Smithsonian Institution
Traveling Exhibition Service (SITES)
Washington, D.C. 20560

Society of American Archaeology
5545 N.E. Skidmore
Portland, Oregon 97218

Society of Architectural Historians
1700 Walnut Street, Suite 716
Philadelphia, Pennsylvania 18103

U.S. Association of Museum Volunteers
1307 New Hampshire Avenue, N.W.
Washington, D.C. 20036

II. U.S. Regional Museum Organizations

Mid-Atlantic Association of Museums
Hope Schladen, Executive Director
P.O. Box 817
Newark, Delaware 19715-0817

Mid-West Museums Conference
c/o Raymond L. Breun, President
Jefferson National Expansion Memorial
11 North 4th Street
St. Louis, Missouri 63102

Mountain-Plains Museum Association
c/o Michael Husband, Director
Old Cowtown Museum
1871 Sem Park Drive
Wichita, Kansas 67203

New England Museums Association
Pam Brusic, Executive Director
c/o Charlestown Navy Yard
Boston National Historical Park
Boston, Massachusetts 02129

Southeastern Museums Conference
c/o Alvin Gerhardt Jr., Director
Rocky Mount Historical Association
Route 2, Box 70
Piney Flats, Tennessee 37686

Western Museums Conference
c/o Dan L. Monroe, President
Portland Art Association
1219 Southwest Park Avenue
Portland, Oregon 97205

III. Regional Conservation Centers in the United States

Balboa Art Conservation Center
P.O. Box 3755
San Diego, California 92103

Center for Conservation and Technical Studies
Fogg Art Museum
32 Quincy Street
Cambridge, Massachusetts 02138

Conservation Center for Art and Historic Artifacts
264 South 23rd Street
Philadelphia, Pennsylvania 19103

Intermuseum Conservation Association
Allen Art Building
Oberlin, Ohio 44074

New York State Office of Parks, Recreation,
and Historic Preservation
Collections Care Center
Peebles Island
Waterford, New York 12188

Northeast Document Conservation Center
Abbott Hall
24 School Street
Andover, Massachusetts 01810

Texas Conservation Center
Panhandle-Plains Historical Museum
Box 967, W.T. Station
Canyon, Texas 79016

Textile Conservation Center
800 Massachusetts Avenue
North Andover, Massachusetts 01845

Pacific Regional Conservation Center
Bishop Museum
P.O. Box 19000-A
Honolulu, Hawaii 96817

Rocky Mountain Regional Conservation Center
2420 South University Boulevard
Denver, Colorado 80208

Upper Mid-West Conservation Association
2400 Third Avenue, South
Minneapolis, Minnesota 55404

Williamstown Regional Art Conservation Laboratory, Inc.
225 South Street
Williamstown, Massachusetts 01267

5

And If You Don't Want to Do All That?

LET'S START AGAIN with the question—who are you?

Are you starting or expanding a museum because you have a collection you'd like to give to the public, or has one been given to your historical society, or have the collections accumulated by your historical society or art league or nature group outgrown the storage and display areas you have at present? In short, are you developing a museum because you have a collection that should be in one?

Well, there is no law that says it has to be in a *new* museum, or even in one of your *own*.

You may save yourself a lot of trouble by checking first to see if an *existing* museum is interested in your collection and has the facilities to give it good care. If you live in Amarillo, Texas, for example, it hardly makes sense to create a new museum there for your collection of ranching equipment when, just a twenty-minute drive away, in Canyon, Texas, the superb Panhandle-Plains Historical Museum already interprets ranching, among other aspects of the region's history, and has a professional staff and good facilities for exhibition and conservation with which to do it. Neither would it make sense to found a new museum of Western art near Tulsa, Oklahoma, where the Gilcrease Institute is already one of the best, or to ignore the fine Museum of Glass in Corning, New York, by establishing a museum nearby for your own glass collection.

Or you may find the best home for your collection by looking far *beyond* your own area. The directories published by the American Association of Museums and the American Association for State and Local History can help you find established museums that specialize in the kind of works of art or historical artifacts or scientific specimens that you have collected or that your organization has inherited. Your handcrafted crystal or rare Spanish spurs or watercolors by painters of the Southeast Coast may be especially valued by museums that long have cared for such things. You may be able to help them fill gaps, making their collections representative and complete in terms of a period of painting, a style of glass work, or an era of ranching history. Instead of setting up a duplicate museum, you might negotiate a gift to them, or a sale or trade, if there are no legal restrictions on disposal of the collection you possess.

At the least, you can do yourself the favor of seeing whether some other museum in your area already exhibits collections like yours. If so, competition for visitors and money is likely to keep both of you weak, making it harder to give your collection proper care.

Another alternative is to consolidate efforts for the benefit of everybody. That is, maybe others in your region have collections for which they are considering new museums, too, or are willing to expand the service area of an existing museum. You might be able to enlist enough cooperation to organize a regional museum, whose board of directors would represent all of you, and whose programs would include traveling exhibits and other museum programs reaching into your town and county as well as others. Such a regional museum could secure a strong financial base, which would assure long-term security for your collection while also providing museum experiences for the area surrounding it, including your community.

Those are some options, if your motive for museum-building is to house collections. But what if you are that Chamber of Commerce person whose motive for a new museum in your community is to attract tourists who will spend money there?

Well, obviously you still have to consider what you will be able to attract them with—that is, what collections you can put in your museum. If you haven't anything special or uniquely relevant to your locality, you aren't likely to draw tourists away from the established museums in your area, anyway. But *if* you have special collections, and *if* you have figured accurately what it costs to create a truly attractive museum and effectively advertise it to tourists, and *if* you are sure that the financial return to your community will cover those costs—fine. There are, however, easier ways to attract visitors with culture.

An annual festival, for example. Many communities draw thousands of visitors to re-enactments or other special commemorations of historical events, or observances of the anniversaries of famous persons, or celebrations of something for which a locality is notable, or crafts demonstrations. Harvest festivals are popular in towns that are recognized for certain agricultural or industrial products. The Spoleto Festival of Music draws visitors from all over the United States to Charleston, South Carolina. The Texas Folklife Festival brings crowds to San Antonio, whose Crockett Hotel organized a national reunion of Davy Crockett's "kin," descendants of the hero of the Alamo. Many communities draw visitors by developing their historic sites or opening their privately owned historic houses for candlelight tours and other festivities.

Good museums sometimes do make great financial contributions to their communities by drawing tourists. But a museum cannot safely risk financial dependence on tourists, and the desire to increase tourism is not, in itself, sufficient to create the kind of museum that really can draw outsiders to the area.

A strong base of local support is essential for sound financing.

What if you are one of those who saved a historic building in your community as a prospect for a museum—and the museum plan fell through? Well, there are lots of other useful things you can do with such a building instead.

Adaptive use of old structures is condoned by historians and preservationists—at least, under certain conditions that can be explained to you by your city's historical commission, your local historic-preservation group, or your state's historic-preservation office. The latter is likely to be in your state's capital city, probably under the state historical society or a government department such as parks or conservation. The federal government helps fund state historic-preservation offices, whose staffs advise citizens about historic-preservation standards, legal restrictions, tax benefits, and sources of financial aid. Also, such advice is available from regional offices as well as the Washington office of the National Trust for Historic Preservation.

Adaptive use of a building means essentially that you keep the building alive and useful in your community by adapting it from its original purpose to something else. Rehabilitating a downtown waterfront warehouse for shops and restaurants is an example, or turning fine old residences into attractive office space. Some historical societies have transformed abandoned railway depots into offices with storage facilities and meeting rooms for themselves.

Such uses may require less extensive—or less expensive—alteration in the interiors of historic buildings than remaking their interiors for secure, climate-controlled, adequately spacious museum use. The old county courthouse may have a wonderful open atrium for exhibits, but that doesn't make it easy or cheap to heat and air-condition uniformly or to re-wire for security, or to re-plumb for a conservation lab, or to make accessible by ramp and elevator for handicapped visitors. You might be better off rehabilitating it for new use as an office building. And rather than becoming a costly rehabilitation for museum purposes, a preserved historic building adapted for commercial use can even be a source of income for a cultural organization. Nonprofit cultural and educational organizations do not necessarily surrender their tax-exempt status by such income-generating activities; they can and do lease space to others in historic properties.

There are alternatives also if you are the park department official who has been asked to use an old building on a historic site for museum exhibits about it. You already know that, unless you have collections, you can't do permanent exhibits. But if you do have collections, that old building may not be adequate for analyzing, recording, storing, conserving, and securing them. Moreover, museum exhibits are not necessarily the best way to explain a site—which, after all, is your real goal. Less complicated, less expensive things can explain the significance of a place to visitors and help them get a feeling of what happened there.

Do you recall, for example, visiting Civil War battlefields or other sites at which the National Park Service had a slide-tape show or movie for orientation to the site, then sent you out with an interpretive brochure for a walking tour, along which you also found big, metal historical markers to explain particular things? Just one or two markers and an inexpensive, illustrated pamphlet can be excellent ways to interpret a small site for visitors. Pamphlets can be reprinted and markers replaced without the kind of perpetual care that museum collections need. And making a slide-tape show can be cheaper than purchasing a genuine Civil War cannon or Revolutionary Army uniform. In fact, improvements in audiovisual technology now make possible wonderfully effective presentations of historical information, nature lore, or aesthetic insight.

Finally, let's consider alternatives if you are contemplating a museum as a lasting way to commemorate a centennial or bicentennial of your community. Isn't your real goal the preservation of your heritage so that it can become better known, understood, and appreciated by the people of your community? A museum is not the only way to accomplish that goal.

Many communities celebrate major anniversaries by publishing books on their history, their natural environment, or the works of art the area may have inspired. States such as New Jersey and Kentucky have produced whole series of books in observance of historical anniversaries. Sometimes historical societies commission history books by professional writers or trained historians at area colleges. In other instances, historical society members collaborate to produce such books, enlisting amateur historians, local newspaper writers, and volunteers for photograph searches.

An increasingly popular kind of anniversary project that can engage a community broadly is oral history, resulting in publications or public programs that share with the community what has been learned from the research. Working under a trained oral historian, or at least using authoritative publications on oral history techniques for interviewing and for evaluating taped testimony, communities can capture the memories of their old-timers and can reconstruct significant events by transcribing and comparing interviews with residents who lived through them.

An especially good example is a project on the Great Depression conducted by the East Tennessee Historical Society in Knoxville. Staff historians there organized volunteers in two counties to interview people who remembered what the Depression was like in their region and to search attics and cellars for letters, photographs, and whatever else survived from the Depression Era. Citizens involved in the project learned about their history by "doing" it themselves. They preserved on tape and in archives much material that otherwise would have been lost about the Depression experience. And they summed up their findings in a permanent written record for generations to come.

Other communities have observed anniversaries by identifying their historic sites and erecting permanent markers about them; by surveying old buildings in neighborhoods for nomination to the National Register of Historic Places; by producing a series of newspaper articles or radio broadcasts or film or television shows on the community's heritage; by revitalizing a historic downtown district under the Main Street Program of the National Trust for Historic Preservation; by sponsoring the excavation and preservation of an archaeological site; by establishing county or city archives as a permanent respository for records and photographs of the locality; by recording headstones in old cemeteries; or by publishing a well-researched guide-map to a region's historic features.

Few communities have done what seems to us the potentially most important thing they could undertake as a special project: a survey of *all* the kinds of historic resources still surviving and available to them. That means checking on the content and condition of anything that may help the community in the future to reconstruct and understand its past—local government records; library collections; newspaper files; photographers' portfolios; historic objects and artifacts that may be moldering away in warehouses, as well as accumulating in private collections; TV and radio tapes; historic buildings and neighborhoods and sites.

Once all such things of historical importance are located, described, and evaluated, then the community can go to work to be sure that the most significant things get saved in the future. And arrangements can be made to secure the most important or valuable kinds of objects, rather than simply whatever happens to survive the ravages of time, so that the significant artifacts will be available in case, just in case, the community should someday decide it really needs and can adequately support, yes, a museum.

For what is important, after all, is not *museums*. What is important is history, art, science—the things we are moved by and enjoy and learn about through the medium of museums. And because no community will ever have enough resources to care completely for everything in its heritage, the wise and prudent thing to do is to identify what is most significant and spend the available money on saving and using that.

A collection of political campaign buttons in a local museum is interesting to look through. But what meaning does it have, if the local election records have been lost, along with the minutes of past council meetings? If there is no photographic or oral-history record of what campaigns used to be like in past periods and how the techniques changed? If newspaper files reporting who won and what the issues were are crumbling? And if the grand old city hall, architectural pride of the community for fifty or a hundred years and seat of its most strident political activity, has itself been torn down to make room for a parking lot?

If, after thinking about all this, a museum still seems to you the best way to serve your love of history, of art, of nature, of heritage, and of your community or group, then please go on to Part II of this book, which will tell you the basic steps in getting a museum going. *But do think about it. Think carefully whether you are ready to accept responsibility for a cultural institution as serious in purpose and complicated in operation as a public library or a school. Do you really want to start a museum?*

For more information

Good ideas for heritage projects are explained in down-to-earth terms in these books:

Nearby History: Exploring the Past Around You, by David E. Kyvig and Myron A. Marty. Nashville, Tennessee: The American Association for State and Local History, 1982. With appendixes, bibliographies, illustrations, and index (300 pages).

A Primer for Local Historical Societies, by Dorothy Weyer Creigh. Nashville: AASLH, 1976. With illustrations and lists of references for other works on such projects as oral history, tours, libraries, publishing, site-marking, and preservation of historic buildings (153 pages).

On different kinds of heritage projects such as those suggested in this chapter, we also recommend the following:

Time Machines: The World of Living History, (217 pages), by Jay Anderson. Nashville: AASLH, 1984.

Information: A Preservation Source Book, with supplements. Washington, D.C.: National Trust for Historic Preservation.

Building to Last: A Handbook on Recycling Old Buildings, (127 pages), by Gene Bunnell. Washington, D.C.: National Trust for Historic Preservation, 1979.

Local History Collections: A Manual for Librarians, (99 pages), by Enid T. Thompson. Nashville: AASLH, 1979.

Historic Preservation in Small Towns, (146 pages), by Arthur P. Ziegler, Jr., and Walter C. Kidney. Nashville: AASLH, 1980.

Architectural Photography, (132 pages), by Jeff Dean. Nashville: AASLH, 1981.

Using Local History in the Classroom, (284 pages), by Fay D. Metcalf and Matthew T. Downey. Nashville: AASLH, 1982.

Researching, Writing, and Publishing Local History, 2nd ed. (166 pages), by Thomas E. Felt. Nashville: AASLH, 1981.

Oral History for the Local Historical Society, 2nd ed. (63 pages) by Willa K. Baum. Nashville: AASLH, 1974.

Transcribing and Editing Oral History, (127 pages), by Willa K. Baum. Nashville: AASLH, 1977.

Videotaping Local History, (160 pages), by Brad Jolly. Nashville: AASLH, 1982.

"Hard Times Remembered: A model community project documents the Depression's impact on two East Tennessee counties," by Charles F. Bryan, Jr., and Mark V. Wetherington, *History News* 39 (August 1984): 28-34.

The following Technical Leaflets from the American Association for State and Local History are also appropriate:

Craft Festivals: A Planning Guide (117), by Daniel Reibel.

Historical Markers: Planning Local Programs (104), by Raymond F. Pisney.

Old Movies: A Source of Local History Programs (100), by Dorothy Weyer Creigh.

History for Young People: Projects and Activities (38), by Doris Platt.

Local Historical Records: Programs for Historical Agencies (121), by Bruce W. Dearstyne.

Concerning local records and persuading your government officials to give them better care, advice is available from NICLOG, the National Information Center for Local Government Records, at AASLH, Nashville, Tennessee, which has publications available and an audiovisual program for rent entitled *Guardians of the Public Record.*

Part II

How Best to Go about It

After a decade of careful planning, the Historical Association of Southern Florida opened its new museum in 1984 in downtown Miami. Veteran museum architect Philip Johnson designed the museum and the cultural center surrounding it. (Photograph by Steven Brooke, courtesy of the Historical Museum of Southern Florida.)

6

Analyze for Essentials

WITH SOME GOOD, solid groundwork outlined, let's put a few things on paper. You'll need a pencil—with a good eraser!—and a pad of paper. From here to the end of this book, we're going to work out, on paper, a mock-up of a sample museum plan. This plan should be made to answer twenty basic questions, four of which we'll cover in each of the next five chapters. We list them here, up front, all at once, so that you can see overall where we're headed:

1. What is your museum's mission and its limits?
2. What sources of support can your museum count on?
3. What collections are available or need to be found to serve your museum's purpose?
4. What physical facilities will work for your museum?
5. Who will have responsibility for the museum?
6. What rules will govern its operations?
7. What divisions of labor and allocations of authority will there be?
8. How will harmonious working relationships be maintained?
9. What will be your collections policy?
10. What conservation needs must you meet and how?
11. What provisions will you make for continuing research?

12. What interpetive methods will you use to reach your public?

13. What time schedule for development will the museum follow?

14. What staff, paid and volunteer, will be needed?

15. What will each part of the plan cost to carry out?

16. Where will the money come from for each?

17. How will you maintain good public relations?

18. How will you provide for continual planning?

19. How will you evaluate your museum's activities?

20. How will you keep your museum alive, dynamic, creative—even visionary?

There's your checklist for planning. And we'll be honest with you about it—we are painfully aware that we can't, in the following short chapters, provide answers to all those questions expertly and in detail. And we well know that what we *can* tell you is easier to say than to do. But we do believe we can tell you enough to show you the overall requirements of museum development, enough at any rate for you to go ahead with confidence that you aren't overlooking essential needs or major problems.

That said, here we go, with *this* chapter's checklist questions—the first four on the list—covering your museum's mission and your potential sources of support, collections, and facilities for carrying that mission out.

First: Now that you have decided to organize a museum, what sort of museum will it be? A Smithsonian of the South? A Metropolitan of the West? Something really grandish, covering everything of significance in art, history, and nature?

Fine—so long as you have the gigantic collections, facilities, and financial support that the Smithsonian has. Those are the essentials. Since—unfortunately—it isn't likely that your initial resources will rival those of the Smithsonian, let's begin with what you really do have and can do. Some possibilities follow, in the form of what museum people call *mission statements:*

• "The purpose of our museum is to preserve for public benefit the natural, historical, and artistic heritage of our region (or state, or city, or county)."

• "The purpose of our museum is to elucidate the history of our community from the time of original inhabitants to the present time."

• "The purpose of our museum is to encourage the fine arts in our area by collecting and exhibiting exemplary works produced here in the past and present."

• "The purpose of our museum is to provide, for the people of our rapidly urbanizing area, an opportunity to remain in touch with nature through maintenance of a green preserve where specimens of our region's plant and animal life are exhibited."

• "The purpose of our museum is to increase understanding and appreciation of the particular heritage of our (ethnic, or racial, or religious) group."

• "The purpose of our museum is to illustrate the history of our (business or industry or other organization)."

• "The purpose of our museum is to preserve, for public education and enjoyment, the Jones Collection of the decorative arts (or whatever)."

All these examples show that no one statement of mission or purpose suits every museum. You will need to analyze your possibilities and write your own mission statement.

Be sure to analyze the *limits* of your intent. To be useful and meaningful, your museum's self-definition must have one particular thing in common with all of those above: it must tell what *limits* the museum will observe.

The limits may be on the kinds of objects collected, the period of history covered, or the group or area whose heritage is to be preserved. Identifying the limits of your intent is necessary to save you from accumulating a haphazard hodgepodge that will confuse your public, eventually overflow your facilities, eat up your resources, and ultimately put your museum at cross-purposes. So, first—and above all else—determine what *limits* you will place on your museum and get that established in a formal mission statement of scope and purpose.

That will become your basic guide to everything else. For example, if you plan a nature-center kind of museum, the old post office you've been offered downtown is obviously not likely to be a useful museum facility. If you intend to illustrate the history of your region, or group, then you aren't going to use your acquisitions budget on even a perfect collection of salt-and-pepper shakers from throughout the world. And if your purpose is to preserve and exhibit a splendid international collection of ceramic vessels, clearly you won't be in the market for stuffed, two-headed calves or Conestoga wagons—and the old post office downtown might suit your museum needs beautifully.

Before making your mission statement an irrevocable document, however, you might well take a prudent intervening step—analyze the *prospects for support*. If the public isn't interested in what your museum will do and be and if no one in your community will contribute the necessary financial backing, *you can have excellent collections and an entirely appropriate building without being able to maintain a museum at all.* And if you have accepted a collection or a building that you can't afford to maintain, you may even be in violation of the public trust laws of your state.

Here's how to analyze potential support for your museum.

First, if you are planning a museum because you've already been offered a collection or a building or both, see whether whoever made the offer—perhaps a wealthy private donor or group—would also contribute an endowment fund to provide for care of the collection or rehabilitation and maintenance of the building. An *endowment fund* is a sum of money for permanent investment, the annual interest from which is used to support a museum's on-going operations and activities. Or if the original donor has given to the limit, would someone else establish an endowment fund?

Remember that the costs of adapting a building or acquiring a collection are only the start of a museum's expenses. Money must also be available for routine costs such as staff salaries, janitorial service, trash hauling, roof repair, heating and air-conditioning, lights, telephones, postage, typewriters and typewriter ribbons, building exhibits, and so on. If no endowment fund is available, or if interest from the one you have won't cover all the probable expenses, then ask whether your city or county or some other unit of government will *appropriate tax or bond funds* annually to support your museum.

If neither endowment funds nor public money will be available or adequate in amount, then *regular, annual fund raising* of some kind will be necessary. What prospects do you have for that? Can you recruit prominent individuals in your community to serve on your museum's board of trustees—people who are willing to contribute funds themselves every year and also persuade others to contribute? Or can you cover your budget from the proceeds of some special, annual fund-raising event? In analyzing those options, take a close look at other nonprofit cultural organizations in your community. How many already support themselves through private fund raising? How well are they doing? If organizations already established are struggling to raise money, filling the community calendar with fund-raising events, or competing for the allegiance of wealthy individuals, how much chance do you have at a piece of the available pie?

Moreover, even if other cultural organizations are succeeding, what *special fund-raising events* might be available to you that they aren't already using? Does the symphony have an annual street fair with food, music, and dancing? Does the historic preservation group organize profit-making tours, travel opportunities, and lecture series? Does the public television station have an antique auction? Do the Boy Scouts and Girl Scouts sponsor benefit performances by popular entertainers? Do the Masonic Lodges sell special newspapers and the veterans' organizations sell lapel flowers? Is the college about to launch another capital-fund drive? If all these cultural, educational, and social service organizations aren't already exhausting the capacity for private giving in your community, what kind of special fund-raising device is left that you can use for the museum?

Part of your analysis should include actually testing the waters. That is, once you've identified a clear public-benefit mission for your museum, you can then try *visiting the kinds of people whose support you'll need*—business leaders, local philanthropists, elected officials, officers of civic clubs, influential newspaper publishers or broadcast executives, and other prominent citizens—to see if they share your enthusiasm and encourage you to seek community support. Additionally, you could even call a countywide or city hall *public meeting,* asking anyone interested in art, science, history, or whatever your museum will promote, to attend to hear about your plans and discuss the pros and cons of your project. Invitations can be extended at large, through news media and posters in store windows, and through special mailings to service clubs and other community groups. If you get the word out well in advance and make the meeting sound interesting, the size of the turnout may itself tell you much about the prospects for your museum.

Among other things, the turnout may help you analyze your chances for supporting the museum through *admission charges* and *membership dues.* Many museums charge entrance fees and attract membership contributions by offering special programs, free passes, or discounts on museum store purchases to members.

Analyze additionally the potential for *contributions of value to the museum besides cash*. Will local lawyers and accountants act as Friends of the Museum and handle the financial and legal needs of the museum without charge? Will lumber yards and hardware dealers donate exhibit-construction material? Will the city or county help at least in providing custodial and security services? Will landscaping firms or garden clubs take care of the museum's grounds? And most important of all, will you be able to recruit an abundance of regular and capable volunteers? Almost no museum operates entirely with paid staff. Almost every museum enlists volunteers to guide visitors, assist with publicity and fund raising, help with research and collections inventories, or whatever else is needed.

Besides a *definition of mission* and an *assessment of sources of support,* the two other essentials that need analysis from the beginning are *collections* and *facilities.* So far, we have more or less assumed that you are starting with one or the other or both. Whether that's true or not, your plan must spell out what you will do about both.

In a later chapter, we'll recommend a formal collections policy. The question now, however, is whether the *collections,* if any, with which you are starting the museum will adequately serve its mission, as you've defined it, or whether a substantial search for suitable objects will be necessary even before you consider opening your doors.

Perhaps you may want to avoid the expense and trouble of caring for your own collections at all. In that event, your plan must identify sources of *traveling exhibits* that will serve the purpose of your museum. Your analysis will include a review of what is available from the SITES program of the Smithsonian Institution (Smithsonian Institution Traveling Exhibition Service), from your state's museum or historical society, and from other museums. Traveling exhibits often are announced in the newsletters of the American Association for State and Local History, the American Association of Museums, and other museum-service organizations. State, provincial, and regional associations of museums also can help you identify what traveling exhibits are available. Some museums do not maintain extensive collections of their own but organize special exhibits through arrangements to borrow temporarily from the collections of others. That approach carries its own problems, such as assuring donor museums of security, insurance, and competence to use their works of art or artifacts safely and meaningfully. If that's what you have in mind, you would be wise to seek guidance from museums that have done it successfully, such as the Museum of Our National Heritage in Lexington, Massachusetts.

More likely, however, you will need to *find collections* suitable for carrying out your particular mission, or you will need to *fill gaps* in such collections as you possess. Is some major artist who worked in your region unrepresented in the collection of regional art you've been given? If your museum's purpose is to show the relationship of the peculiarities of your region's climate and environment to the kinds of plant and animal life that exist there, do you have enough specimens or pictorial material on birds, fish, insects, and so forth, to do that? For your history museum, what kinds of things were significant in each phase of your region's development, or representative of life in each period? What is still available to illustrate river transport, railroads, farming, mining, business and industry, labor, churches, schools, cultural institutions, ethnic communities, costumes, pastimes, government and politics, social relations? In short, for whatever kind of museum you plan to establish, how much *additional* collecting will you need to do?

Finally, what about adequate *facilities?*

Whether you are building a new structure for a museum or

adapting an old one, analysis begins with a list of each kind of activity you may need to carry on within it. Does your facility have space for offices, storage of collections, storage of supplies and maintenance materials, exhibits, a meeting room, shops for fabrication of exhibits and for cleaning and conservation of objects, a kitchen for such uses as catering receptions, an archive and research library, space for training volunteers, an audiovisual theater, and maybe a gift shop? Above all, save yourself from the initial mistake of supposing that exhibit space is the primary consideration. *Storage and work areas* should equal or exceed exhibit space. The rule of thumb for allocation of space in museum structures is 40 percent for exhibits, 40 percent for storage, and 20 percent for offices and other activities.

Knowing that, now analyze the *utility of the space* in any building you may be offered. A superb Victorian mansion, for example, may have room divisions that present serious problems for exhibit presentations, flow of visitor traffic, and security. High ceilings and lots of windows may make it difficult or expensive to maintain the proper ranges of temperature and relative humidity or the protection from direct sunlight that museum collections, on exhibit or in storage, need to prevent deterioration. Structural changes needed to solve those problems may run afoul of historic preservation standards—a historic structure is itself a valuable artifact that requires handling with an eye to maintaining the integrity of its historical and architectural character. It would not be historically helpful to make more space for an exhibit about President Lincoln in the old Ford Theater in Washington, D.C., by tearing out the theater box where he was sitting when shot.

If at all possible, *enlist both an architect and an experienced museum professional* to help you analyze an existing building for problems that may cause you grief and cost you money if you don't deal with them before starting a museum operation. Does the roof need replacing? Is the building made of something such as masonry that may enable you to use it for a museum for at least fifty to a hundred years? Is there insulation in it that will hold down utility bills? Can the wall surfaces be easily cleaned and used for museum purposes? Will the floor coverings long survive several thousand visitors a year, tracking in mud and moisture from rain and snow? Can the climate be controlled with affordable air conditioning and heating units? Does the electrical wiring meet commercial standards and government codes? Are there enough circuits for lighting exhibits, galleries, offices, and program areas as well as outside lights, security systems, evening receptions and programs, and shop equipment, without risking blown fuses or fires? Is the plumbing adequate for public restrooms and water fountains, as well as for the kitchen? What about the paint? Surfaces need to be attractive but also easy to clean and maintain. Please avoid the assumption, however, that a history museum *has* to be in an *old* building. Unused space in a brand-new, reflective-glass-and-steel building is just as acceptable for history museums as it is for others. Whatever kind of museum you plan, a *new building* can more readily be made to suit your needs—but again, only if you analyze them carefully. Ideally, you will choose an architect who has museum-design experience. Since such architects are few, we recommend that you look for one who at least is willing to study the special problems of museum design in consultation with museum professionals.

What construction material will the architect recommend? Wood siding, composition shingles, and wood decking are neither cheap to buy nor easy to maintain. Masonry construction lasts longer. How long do you want the structure to serve your museum? Can the architecture of the building itself express the museum's nature and purpose? Can it relate harmoniously to the architecture of nearby buildings and the character of the neighborhood around it? Can site planning allow for possible future expansion, along with adequate access, control of traffic patterns, and ample parking or proximity to public transportation? Will the design enable visitors to be monitored easily in the exhibit areas but also to get out readily in case of fire or other natural disaster? Those are all important questions to ask your architect.

One final word of caution: It's easy to think of the building as the museum itself and invest the bulk of your resources in what is only *housing for collections and programs.* Be sure your budgeting takes both these essential expenditures into consideration early on.

So—now you know what essentials must be analyzed as the first part of your plan. You are ready to start answering these questions in the check-list for your museum plan:

1. What is your museum's mission and its limits?
2. What sources of support can your museum count on?
3. What collections are available or need to be found to serve your museum's purpose?
4. What physical facilities will work for your museum?

For more information

Of relevance to subjects in this chapter, we recommend the following publications:

Thoughts on Museum Planning and *Thoughts on the Museum and the Community,* by the Museum and Field Service Department of the Texas Historical Commission, published in 1976 by the Commission and the Texas Historical Foundation in Austin, Texas.

Technical Leaflets, published by the American Association for State and Local History:

Financing Your History Organization: Setting Goals (106), by Laurence R. Pizer.

Recruiting Members for Your Historical Society (37), by Daniel Porter.

Collecting Historical Artifacts: An Aid for Small Museums (6), by Eugene F. Kramer.

Before Restoration Begins: Keeping Your Historic House Intact (62), by Henry A. Judd.

Museum News Reprints, published by the American Association of Museums, Washington, D.C.:

Development: Building a Sound Financial Base for Museums (series of articles written by members of the Art Museum Development Association).

What Architects Need to Know, and Don't Want to Hear, by John Hilberry.

Museum Collections Storage, by John Hilberry and Susan Kalb Weinberg.

Museums and Adaptive Use, articles from the September 1980 issue of *Museum News* on using old buildings to house museums.

For those contemplating new buildings, we suggest obtaining from the American Institute of Architects, 44 Industrial Park Drive, P.O. Box 753, Waldorf, Maryland 20601, a publication entitled *Selecting Architects for Public Projects* (16 pages), by the AIA staff.

For help in understanding and evaluating the usefulness of historical collections, we recommend *Artifacts and the American Past* (294 pages), by Thomas J. Schlereth, published in 1980 by AASLH, Nashville, Tennessee. Also, useful for architectural planning, among other things, is *The Technical Requirements of a Small Museum* (27 pages), by Raymond O. Harrison, Canadian Museums Association, Ottawa, Ontario, Canada.

Useful for assessing funding prospects are these publications:

Gifts of Property: A Guide for Donors and Museums, a 25-page pamphlet published in 1985 by the Association of Art Museum

Directors and the American Association of Museums, and available from the latter in Washington, D.C.

Discover Total Resources: A Guide for Nonprofits, a 44-page booklet published in 1985 by the Community Affairs Division of the Mellon Bank, One Mellon Bank Center, Pittsburgh, Pennsylvania 15285.

The Gallier House, a historic house museum in New Orleans's famed French Quarter, features an enclosed, nineteenth-century garden. (Photograph courtesy of the Gallier House.)

7

Organize for Operation

Now that you've specified your museum's mission and made plans for its collections, facilities, and support, you are ready to plan the operating organization. You can begin to answer the checklist questions about rules and responsibilities, divisions of labor and authority, and harmonious working relations. You know enough of what the museum will be and do to draft its constitution and bylaws.

Those may not necessarily be the terms you use. *Constitutions* with bylaws are usually the governing documents of museums that are organized, operated, and primarily supported by groups of private citizens. We strongly recommend that such museums incorporate under the laws of their state as not-for-profit, tax-exempt corporations, in which case the *articles of incorporation* may become the basic governing document. If the museum belongs to a county or municipality, its governing document may be the *ordinance* by which the county or city council establishes it. If some other governing body, such as a college or university, creates the museum, its governing document may be a *charter* that grants specified rights and powers from and within the larger organization.

All such documents, however, serve essentially the same purposes and cover essentially the same issues. They define the museum, authorize its operation, and describe the way in which power will be organized, exercised, and limited within the institution. Such a governing document must be established in accordance with federal, state, and local laws, and must be adopted formally by whatever duly constituted body will have authority for the museum—a city or county council, a university board of regents, the group of original incorporators, or whoever else will take legal responsibility for the museum. And once adopted, the governing document should have the force of law in the museum's operations.

We recommend that you retain a competent attorney—if you can't find free legal assistance—to draft your governing document. Knowledge of the law will help, particularly with parts of the document that establish the legal existence of the organization, authorize its perpetual operation, describe the limits of liability of its trustees or members, specify its tax status, declare its right to hold property and receive gifts, and provide for what will happen to its assets if it should go out of operation.

We also urge you to apply for *tax-exempt status* from the U.S. Internal Revenue Service under the federal internal revenue code (or in Canada from the Department of Internal Revenue), particularly if your museum wants to attract donations of collections and cash. Designation by the IRS as a tax-exempt educational or charitable organization not only saves your museum from having to pay federal taxes, but also allows donors to your museum to reduce their income tax payments by a portion of the monetary value of their gifts. That is a powerful incentive for businesses and individuals to make gifts. They can contribute to the cultural enrichment of their own communities while also reducing their personal tax liabilities. They can't take "charitable deductions," however, for gifts to a museum, unless that museum has tax-exempt approval from the IRS. The internal revenue code specifies that museums can avoid paying taxes themselves and can assure donors of tax write-offs for their gifts *only* if they are "organized and operated exclusively for one or more of the purposes enumerated as allowed by the federal regulations governing tax-exempt organizations." Therefore, your constitution, charter, articles of incorporation, or enabling ordinance should specify that your museum is serving one or more of those purposes. For lists of those purposes, forms, and other information about applying for tax-exempt status, contact your area's IRS office or check your telephone book for a toll-free number for the Internal Revenue Service.

What else should be in the basic *governing document*? Typically, it contains articles or paragraphs answering these questions:

1. What is the name of the corporation or organization and its general nature (including nonprofit status)?
2. What are its purposes?
3. Where is it incorporated or chartered and what is its offical location?
4. How is it governed, including provision for officers and trustees?
5. What specific powers will it have, such as the power to receive gifts, hold property, enter into contracts, appoint agents and employees, and carry out activities?
6. By what procedure can the governing document be amended?

Depending on state legal requirements, a governing document may also include authorization of public notary, the intended duration of the organization, the names and addresses of its incorporators or organizers and any registered agents they may have, provisions for membership, and a dissolution clause providing for the disposition of assets in the event that the museum ceases operation.

In addition to the primary governing document, most museums also have *bylaws* that provide more procedural detail, particularly about things that are more likely to need change from time to time. Bylaws typically spell out the roles and responsibilities of governing boards and of individuals who will carry out the board's policies, such as a director or other paid or volunteer staff. A museum's bylaws typically follow this outline:

1. Name of the museum and governing organization
2. Purpose(s)
3. Board of Directors (trustees, or equivalent policy-setting body)
   a. Number, qualifications, and terms of office
   b. Nomination and election procedures
   c. Removal procedures
   d. Filling of vacancies
   e. Place, time, number, and requirements for announcing meetings
   f. Quorum requirements
   g. Committees
4. Officers
   a. Number and method of election or selection
   b. Powers and duties
   c. Removal procedures
5. Members (if any)
   a. Classifications
   b. Dues and benefits
   c. Meetings and provisions for notice and a quorum
6. Advisory Bodies (if any)
   a. Appointment procedures and requirements
   b. Powers and duties
7. Financial Provisions
   a. Definition of fiscal year
   b. Authority to sign checks and transfer funds
   c. Authority to enter contracts
   d. Authority to accept gifts and donations

e. Budget preparation and financial reporting requirements

8. Amendment Procedures

Let us repeat—constitutions and bylaws are not window dressing or mere legal formalities. You'll suffer if you put anything into governing documents that you don't intend to live by. And it helps to draft such documents as clearly and precisely as you can, so that those who will be legally responsible under them can understand their requirements unmistakably from the outset.

In the bylaws—or in additions to them—take special care to make clear the difference between the *responsibilities of trustees* and the *responsibilities of staff,* whether staff members are paid or volunteer. More conflict arises in museums from failure to understand and respect the division between the role of trustees and of the staff director than from any other cause, partly because it is hard to draw absolutely clear lines defining the separate categories of duties.

The standard distinction is that *the board sets policy, which the staff carries out.* For example, the board approves a proposal from the staff director to create a new exhibit, and the board authorizes expenditures for it as part of the annual budget. Staff should respect the right of the board to say yes or no to a major expenditure for such a purpose. But if the board does authorize the exhibit, *then board members should let the staff create it,* using that professional judgment for which the board hired the staff. A staff director or curator who goes ahead with a major exhibit that the board rejected or did not provide for within the approved budget is exceeding his or her authority. On the other hand, a board member who walks into the museum and proceeds to tell staff which artifacts to use in an approved exhibit, how to design it, what to put on the labels, and what printing firm to hire to make them is overstepping the bounds of a trustee's role. Also, the staff director needs a free hand to hire and fire personnel; that should not be a prerogative of the board. The board is entitled to hold the director responsible for whatever good or harm any of the staff may do.

The staff director should be held accountable for the budget and responsible for the quality of the museum within budget restrictions. But the director cannot produce quality work within budgetary limitations without the freedom to make disbursements, choose vendors, and exercise judgment about how to achieve quality in an authorized activity. If the board gives the director full authority to carry out approved activities and then is not happy with the quality of the results, the board has every right to replace the director.

That is true whether the director is paid or volunteer. It's easy on the budget to let some talented citizen or even an unpaid member of the board provide day-to-day administrative direction. But such volunteers can thumb their noses at boards more easily than professionals dependent on salaries. And all too often an individual with great energy and enthusiasm volunteers to run a museum for a board that is relieved to turn it over to someone—anyone—with the result that the museum eventually gets the image of belonging to that dedicated individual, who begins to confuse himself or herself with the board and insists on deciding unilaterally what to do as well as doing it. As more people feel ignored and excluded, a "mom-and-pop" museum eventually loses public interest and support.

On the other hand, particularly when the staff director is able and energetic, trustees often begin to expect him or her to do even the things for which trustees have particular responsibility. Helping to organize a lobbying effort or a fund-raising campaign is an appropriate staff activity but the trustees are ultimately responsible for securing the necessary funds. They are the people with influence who can ask others for money.

The old cliche is that members of a museum board should follow the "three G's—give, get, or get off." No board will be able to keep competent staff long if, every year, the director alone has to go out and in effect raise his or her own salary.

In museums so small that no professional staff has yet been hired—or museums that have, at most, a paid director—boards sometimes designate *committees* to help carry out such activities as publicity, acquisitions for the collections, or even exhibit preparation and special programs, as well as fund-raising. Even in those instances, however, final authority for decisions about ways to carry out an approved project should be vested in an individual who is designated as administrator of the museum, even if unpaid.

A wise director will know how to exercise such authority without seeming dictatorial to committee chairs and members. And a wise director will keep the board well informed on the progress of all activities, as well as alerted to anything that *isn't* going well or is potentially controversial or dangerous. A wise board, particularly its president or chairperson, will regularly review the quality of the museum's activities and will let the director know of any concern about his or her performance at the earliest convenient moment after that concern arises. More than one board president has felt unduly excluded from the museum's activities by a director who preferred to operate in the dark. And more than one director has been dismissed before receiving any inkling that the board was upset about anything. Candid, open communication, even when opinions are in conflict, is the best guarantee of ultimate harmony.

There's room for give and take in parceling out roles and responsibilities. The standard practices can be modified by negotiation. But it's imperative that officers, board members, paid staff, and volunteers all clearly understand the rules, whatever they are—who has authority to do what, and who will be held responsible for the results. The board itself should see that the rules are followed by its own members, as well as by the staff.

Planning an operating organization goes beyond codifying the rules in a constitution and bylaws, charter, or ordinance. We recommend that you plan also to have *special meetings,* particularly once the museum is operational, for the purpose of going over the governing documents, raising and resolving questions of authority and responsibility, and particularly orienting new board members or staff directors to the expectations of the organization. There's nothing quite like a cocktail party or a reception to provide a warm, friendly, human setting for introducing a newcomer to the board or staff and outlining the ground rules.

With that, the organizational part of your planning begins, and you start answering the four questions on our planning checklist that deal with operating the museum:

5. Who will have responsibility for the museum?

6. What rules will govern its operations?

7. What divisions of labor and allocations of authority will there be?

8. How will harmonious working relationships be maintained?

For more information

More detail on the legal things that museums must worry about or make provision for may be found in these publications:

Museums and the Law (AASLH Museum Management Series, vol.I), by Marilyn Phelan, J.D. (287 pages). Nashville: The American Association for State and Local History, 1983.

A Legal Primer on Managing Museum Collections, by Marie C.

Malaro (351 pages). Washington, D.C.: The Smithsonian Institution Press, 1985.

More information on trustee responsibilities and relations with staff may be found in these publications:

Museum Trusteeship, by Alan D. Ullberg with Patricia Ullberg (130 pages). Washington, D.C.: American Association of Museums, 1981.

Of Mutual Respect and Other Things: An Essay on Museum Trusteeship, by Helmuth J. Naumer (31 pages). Washington, D.C.: American Association of Museums, 1977.

Personnel Policies for Museums: A Handbook for Management, by Ronald L. Miller (164 pages). Washington, D.C.: American Association of Museums, 1977.

Museum Ethics, by the Committee on Ethics of AAM (31 pages). Washington, D.C.: American Association of Museums, 1978.

A 1910 vintage kitchen exhibit acquaints visitors to the Museum of Western Colorado in Grand Junction with one aspect of the region's history. (Photograph by Jerry Van Wyngarden, courtesy of the Museum of Western Colorado.)

8

Plan for Activities

"AHA," you may be thinking; "I've gone through all the complicated analysis and organizational stuff. I have a mission for my museum. I've located collections and facilities. I've arranged for support. I've set up an organization ready to go operational. At least on paper, I've done all that. Now we can deal with the fun things, right? Programs, exhibit openings, receptions, champagne?!"

Well, not quite. We're not really ready yet for a flashy public event or a grand unveiling. First come provisions for the continuing functions that are essential for everything a museum presents to its public. The on-going activities are what now need to be added to your plan. So in this chapter we will deal with the checklist questions about collecting, conservation, research, and interpretation.

First: *Collecting.*

Please sharpen your pencil, because your plans for collecting are going to require another document. A written *collections policy* is essential. Indeed, it is almost as important as your museum's constitution or other basic governing document. Its greatest value is to give clear direction to an active plan for building your collections. The collections policy is also a tool for sticking with your mission statement against a lot of otherwise confusing pressures.

For example, suppose your museum's formally established

89

mission is to preserve evidence of the history of your city. But then, one day, your Uncle Ned comes in, with a big-hearted look, to announce that, in church last Sunday, he realized he should give the museum all the mounted wild-animal heads he has been accumulating from years of summer-time safaris. And what do you say to that? Well, not only are they more relevant to Kenya than to your city, but also they'll take up more room than anything else you have, and the expense of repairing the more moth-eaten ones will drain staff time and money for professional taxidermy. But how can you refuse good-hearted Uncle Ned?

What do you do when one of your museum's trustees wants to give you a collection of excellent paintings by a fine nineteenth-century artist who concentrated on scenes of your city? The trustee will give you this collection, that is, if you will sign an inflated appraisal of the paintings' monetary value, so that the trustee can get a substantial tax write-off.

What do you do if, ten years after a businessman has given his exquisite, locally made furniture to your museum, his heirs decide they want the collection back and claim it was only on loan? What do you do if you find the president of your museum's board either borrowing a piece of that fine furniture for use at home, or throwing some of it away because he or she thinks it's space-consuming and ugly?

In all those instances, you can say, "No, I'm sorry, I'd like to help you, but it's against the museum's collections policy." But you can do that *only*, of course, if you *have* a written, board-endorsed collections policy.

Often, when a group begins to operate a museum, one of the great temptations is to accept any old or valuable object, just to fill exhibit space. But a museum is not a community attic, and most particularly it is not a depository for white elephants— things people don't want but can't bear to throw away. So the collections policy starts with your mission statement and then spells out the kinds of things the museum wants and doesn't want, outlines what procedure must be followed for deciding whether to accept a gift or approve a purchase, and specifies what procedure must be followed for discarding anything or letting it for any reason leave the museum—rules for *deaccessioning,* as museum people call it. Sometimes, museums specify that the director or a special acquisitions or collections committee, or the entire governing board of the museum, must formally approve before any object can be accepted, purchased, sold, traded, lent, thrown out, or given away. That helps prevent hanky-panky, jiggery-pokery, or arbitrary action by any individual staff member or trustee, along with intramural theft, negligence, or bad judgment. It also helps prevent hurt feelings, angered former supporters, and even lawsuits.

Trouble with the Internal Revenue Service can be avoided if the collections policy forbids anyone connected with the museum to appraise the value of gifts for tax purposes. There is nothing wrong with encouraging donors to recognize the legitimate tax benefits to which they may be entitled if they give valuable objects, but they should be referred to *independent,* expert appraisers—people not connected with the museum. Collections policies also can reduce conflict-of-interest problems by forbidding staff members to collect personally, or traffic in, the same kinds of objects that the museum collects.

As a general rule, we also recommend that the collections policy forbid accepting objects if donors place conditions on the use or ultimate disposition of those objects. Fewer disputes are likely if material is accepted on loan only for brief, specified periods of time, for use in some special exhibit or study. Otherwise, the museum should seek full title to anything it accepts or purchases, including the right to dispose of the item by sale, trade, or whatever, at the museum's discretion. Of course, donors will be more likely to make unrestriced gifts of valuable material if they know the museum has a formal collections policy that will prevent arbitrary treatment of what the donor is giving.

Additionally, the museum should avoid gifts that come with restrictions that limit the museum's ability to exhibit effectively. Gifts can give a museum future headaches if donors insist that all items in their collections be forever displayed together, or that a donated artifact be put on permanent exhibit, or that the donor's name be perpetually displayed in a prominent way with the exhibit. So the collections policy should also identify *unacceptable restrictions on gifts*.

Finally, the collections policy should specify what is to be done once an item is accepted. When an object arrives, formal record-keeping needs to begin. An *accession sheet* (see Appendix B) will identify the source and nature of each new object or collection, following which condition evaluations and documentary research should proceed as soon as possible. *Registration* is what museum people call this kind of record-keeping. Without it, things will be as hard to keep track of in the museum as they are in the average basement or attic, and individual trustees or staff members are likely to be playing house whimsically with collections. When somebody from your state attorney general's office arrives to check on your compliance with public-trust statutes, you'll need to be able to pull a file or punch a computer button that will identify each object you have, tell where it is, summarize what is known about it, specify where and how you got it, and under what conditions, tell what shape it is in, what conservation treatment it needs or has been given, and what uses you have made of it to date, including use in exhibits.

Because museums differ, no one collection policy should absolutely duplicate any other. Each policy should, however, at the minimum, spell out rules for acquisitions (accepting gifts and loans and making purchases), for deaccessioning (removing objects in any way from the museum), and for control of collections (arrangements for their registration, care, and use). Ideally, a collections policy might cover all the following:

1. Acquisition policies and procedures
2. Documentation and care procedures
3. Loan and borrowing provisions
4. Security and insurance
5. Access and disclosure commitments and conditions
6. Ethics to be observed by staff and trustees
7. Deaccessison rules

Once the collecting-policy document establishes rules and procedures, then the *collecting plan* may go forward. And that means deciding, on the basis of your mission and the collections already available to you, how much and what kinds of additional material you need to seek, who will do it, where, and over what period of time. Your goal may be to fill in gaps in a representative collection of regional artists, to acquire specimens of plant life to round out other natural-history collections, or to bring your history collection up into the twentieth century. How specifically can you identify the material you hope to add within the next three to five years, and the ways in which you'll go about it?

"Okay," you may be saying, "fine—obviously, we need collections to do exhibits, so we'll plan a collections policy and a collecting plan. *Now* can we go on to exhibits?'

Well, you can—unless you don't want the objects you put into your exhibits to crumble, fade, rust, warp, or otherwise disintegrate before your very eyes and the eyes of your visitors. Because that's what will happen if you don't first plan *conservation* activities.

Conservation, too, is an on-going function, because whether your collections are in storage, being studied, on exhibit, or otherwise in use, they need protection from insects, extremes of and fluctuations in temperature and relative humidity, excessive levels of light, airborne pollutants, deliberate or inadvertent vandalism, or any one of a number of other things, depending on the materials of which the artifact is made. Because artifacts are different in the care they need, and because repairs and protective treatments can themselves be damaging if ordinary household remedies are followed rather than scientific conservation techniques, a conservation program may be difficult for the non-professional to plan. In that case, what you should do is plan to obtain expert advice.

The professional you may hire to direct your museum or any experienced museum person you engage as a consultant should be able to help you plan good, general, overall protective conditions for your collections, including methods and procedures for evaluating the physical condition of each object when you get it and then periodically thereafter, particularly before and after you have used it. If your museum becomes big enough, your collections and budget may warrant hiring a trained professional conservator on your own staff. But at least in the beginning, other arrangements can be made for expert treatment of objects in your collection that are in bad shape or in danger of rapid deterioration. Large museums in your area may have scientific conservators who can help, or you may seek assistance from one of the regional conservation centers in the United States (see list at end of chapter 4). Your state museum association or state historical society probably can identify the one nearest you. Also some trained conservators are sometimes private practitioners available for consultant or treatment jobs.

"Very well," you say; "we'll plan to get expert assistance to meet our conservation needs. So now let's go on to exhibits."

We say, fine—if you can answer the following questions: Can you prove that the paintings you are putting up on the museum wall are genuinely the work of a celebrated artist? Are you sure those bones you are displaying are a prehistoric mastodon's, rather than some over-sized, more recent mule's? How did those mounted butterflies live and reproduce and relate to the rest of your environment? And what change did trolley cars, like that one you are pushing into the museum, make in the development of your city?

In short, do you really know anything about the objects you've assembled to exhibit?

To keep your museum from simply spreading misinformation or trivia, please also plan for continuing *research*. Research means asking owners or donors everything they know about an object when it comes into the museum, then checking that information with other sources. It means documenting the basic facts about what an object is, while also studying the historical, artistic, or scientific context—the larger picture—into which the object fits, and which illuminates its significance. It means proving that your museum's old rifle really is a .45-caliber Springfield used in the U.S. Army after the Civil War. It also means finding out what this kind of weapon in general, and this rifle specifically, had to do with the Winning of the West.

Neither research nor collections themselves are very useful, of course, unless catalogued. That is, each object in your collections and all the information you have on it needs to be accessible, so you can find it when you need it for an exhibit, a research report, or an educational program. Thus cataloguing collections is a major museum function. *Cataloguing* means organizing information on items in the collections by categories, so that when you need to know something about the guns in your collection, for example, you can find it under *Firearms,* or products made by the *Springfield Armory,* or artifacts associated with the *Plains Indians Wars*. Increasingly, museums use computers to store and retrieve information on their collections, but manual card catalogues like the familiar ones seen in libraries can also be used. Museums typically maintain separate accession files, donor files, and object files. Examples of forms and different systems for registering and cataloguing museum objects may be found in established museums and in books such as those cited at the end of this chapter.

Your plan needs to specify *who will do research and cataloguing*. Will it be members of the staff? A research committee of volunteers or board members? Expert faculty in local colleges and universities? Students under supervision of teachers or museum staff? It should be whoever is knowledgeable and appropriate. Also you need to plan *research facilities*—a museum library of reference materials related to your collections. And remember that part of the pleasure and satisfaction of on-going research activity is that new facts will continue to turn up, new insights will become possible and, accordingly, old interpretations may need revision.

And now, we *are* ready for exhibits—almost!

Almost, because exhibits are only part of what we are ready for. Exhibits are one vehicle for a continuing activity called *interpretation*. Interpretation, essentially, is what you say about your collections in both speaking and writing, to coax your public to learn from and appreciate your museum. You may want to interpret through several coordinated means of reaching the public.

Suppose you yourself are simply a unit of that public living near a museum that has a multifaceted interpretive program. You've probably encountered museum interpretation without even going to the museum. There you are, listening to the radio on the way home from work, when you hear a fascinating discussion about life in an earlier era in your community. It is part of a series of weekly broadcasts produced by the community museum. Stopping at the shopping center, you find, in a storefront, an exhibit of the kinds of things that a general store would have offered its customers in your city a hundred years ago—or seventy—or thirty-five—with a label about merchandising methods, compliments of the community museum. Reaching home, you turn on the television and somebody from the educational station is showing different kinds of early-day farm implements from the collections of the museum and explaining how they were used. And in the evening paper, there's an article by the museum director about a regional artist whose watercolor landscapes have just been acquired by the museum.

Suddenly you're interrupted, however, by Junior, who wants to tell you all about the special trip the fifth grade took by bus that day. Where? To the museum. "We learned all about the kinds of animals we used to have around here! Do you know how to tell poisonous from nonpoisonous snakes? Do you know that we used to have buffalo?" Which reminds you—isn't somebody supposed to speak about the area's ecology, past and present, at Rotary or the Garden Club this week? Somebody from the museum.

Maybe, you decide, you just better go see this place.

So, the next day, you go to visit the museum building itself. At the entrance, a person gives you a brochure that tells you what is on exhibit. This person also asks if you'd like the guided tour, available in half an hour. If so, you can first sit in the museum's modest theater and see an audiovisual program on the history of the community, made from the museum's collection of old photographs. Or, if you want to tour the exhibits without a live guide, the person says, you might want to borrow a "take-with-you" gadget with earphones that will tell you about what you're seeing as you walk.

You decide to wait. But on your way to the audiovisual theater, you notice an alcove where the museum sells publications, and they look fascinating. There is a book—an illustrated history of your community, published by the museum. There are catalogues depicting different exhibits the museum has presented. There are copies of the museum's monthly newsletter, containing articles about different objects in the museum, along with announcements of lectures, films, and other special programs.

Publications, audiovisual productions, guided tours, self-guiding tours—through electronic devices and pamphlets—lectures, films, school programs, presentations to community groups, traveling exhibits, newspaper articles, programs on radio and TV—all these things can be parts of the museum's overall interpretive program, and you haven't even reached the exhibits yet!

Well, planning interpretive activities obviously means deciding which of the many possible devices you want to use to extend the educational reach of your collections. Also, you may plan to coordinate these devices with each other, publishing catalogues when you open new exhibits, for example, or creating traveling displays to meet curricular needs of school programs. And as for exhibits, some can be *permanent*, such as those that tell the basic story of your community, and others can be temporary, such as a six-month special show on some particular group, event, or facet of life in your region. And from time to time you may plan to bring in traveling exhibits from other museums as well. Now you can even plan receptions for new exhibit openings!

Exhibit preparation itself, however, like every one of the other interpretive activities named above, takes special planning. It is really an art, requiring imaginative combinations of artifacts with well-written labels, graphic material, and attractive layouts or showcases. Sound, light, and color all may enhance the effect of an exhibit, or detract from the artifacts, the originals—the "real things"—if not sensitively handled. Also, *too much* information can frustrate visitors as badly as too little.

It's possible that, to be really good, exhibits might be the last part of your museum plan to be carried out. Or you might begin by offering only some temporary or introductory kinds of exhibits to whet the interest of your public as you get the rest of the museum's programs in place. But don't forget the other ways through which to share appreciation of your collections as well. Or the collecting, conservation, and research that are essential for you to have anything significant to share.

We've not been able to tell you much here about how to do all these things; but at least you know that programming of any kind requires answering these four questions in your basic checklist for planning:

9. What will be your collections policy?

10. What conservation needs must you meet and how?

11. What provisions will you make for on-going research?

12. What interpretive methods will you use to reach your public?

For more information

On collections policies and plans, we recommend:

Current Thoughts on Collections Policy: Producing the Essential Document for Administering Your Collections (12 pages), by Daniel Porter, Technical Report 1, Technical Information Service, AASLH, Nashville, Tennessee.

On conservation of collections, we recommend these publications:

Thoughts on Museum Conservation (35 pages). Austin: Texas Historical Commission and the Texas Historical Foundation, 1976.

Basic Principles for Controlling Environmental Conditions in Museums and Historical Agencies (16 pages), by Shelley Reisman Paine, Technical Report 3, AASLH Technical Information Service.

The Care of Antiques and Historical Collections (248 pages), by

A. Bruce MacLeish. Nashville: AASLH, 1985.

A Handbook on the Care of Painting, revised ed. (136 pages), by Caroline Keck. Nashville: AASLH, 1967.

A Primer on Museum Security, by Caroline Keck and others. Cooperstown: New York State Historical Association, 1966.

"Security Checklist for the Small Museum," by Jack Leo, in *History News* 35 (June 1980).

On museum record-keeping, we recommend these publications:

Registration Methods for the Small Museum (160 pages), by Daniel Reibel. Nashville: AASLH, 1978.

Museum Registration Methods, 3rd ed., (437 pages), by Dorothy Dudley, Irma Bezold Wilkinson, and others. Washington D.C.: American Association of Museums, 1979.

On various interpretive programs, including exhibits, we recommend these publications:

Thoughts on Museum Interpretation(12 pages). Austin: Texas Historical Commission and Texas Historical Foundation, 1977.

History by Design: A Primer on Interpreting and Exhibiting Community History (77 pages), by Patrick Norris. Austin: Texas Association of Museums, 1985.

Interpretation of Historic Sites, 2nd ed. (202 pages), by William T. Alderson and Shirley Payne Low. Nashville: AASLH, 1985.

Exhibits for the Small Museum: A Handbook (169 pages), by Arminta Neal. Nashville: AASLH, 1976.

Help! for the Small Museum (200 pages), by Arminta Neal. Boulder, Colo.: Pruett Publishing, 1969.

Good Show! A Practical Guide for Temporary Exhibitions (172 pages), by Lothar P. Witteborg. Washington, D.C.: SITES Program, Smithsonian Institution, 1981.

On tours and school programs in particular, we recommend these Technical Leaflets from the American Association for State and Local History, Nashville, Tennessee:

Historic Houses as Learning Laboratories: Seven Teaching Strategies (105), by Thomas J. Schlereth.

Training for Docents: How to Talk to Visitors (125), by Gerald H. Krockover and Jeanette Hauck.

Planning Museum Tours: For School Groups (93), by Richard Vanderway.

On understanding artifacts for all interpretive-program purposes, we recommend these short publications:

Designing Your Exhibits: Seven Ways to Look at an Artifact, by Fred Schroeder, AASLH Technical Leaflet 91, AASLH, Nashville, Tennessee.

Interpreting and Reinterpreting Associative Historic Sites and Artifacts, (16 pages), by Fred E. H. Schroeder, Technical Report 6, Technical Information Service, AASLH, Nashville, Tennessee.

"Things Unspoken: Learning Social History from Artifacts," by Barbara G. Carson and Cary Carson, in *Ordinary People and Everyday Life: Perspectives on the New Social History,* edited by James B. Gardner and George Rollie Adams. Nashville: AASLH, 1983.

"The Link from Object to Person to Concept," by James Deetz, in *Museums, Adults, and the Humanities: A Guide for Educational Programming,* edited by Zapporah W. Collins. Washington, D.C.: American Association of Museums, 1981.

A plaster figure of a farmer plows with his No. 13 Oliver Chilled Plow at the Discovery Hall Museum in South Bend, Indiana. (Photograph courtesy of the Discovery Hall Museum.)

9

Set Up the Resources

THE PRELIMINARY PLANNING is nearly finished. The last chapter dealt with identifying on-going activities and special programs for your museum—the things you really are going to do. Completing the plan requires providing for people, money, and time to do those things. What human and financial resources will your program plans require? And on what schedule? For *time* is a resource, too. Your plan will need to show what your museum will do, who will do it, how you will finance it, and when all this is to take place.

For example, you might set up a *three-year plan*, culminating in the public opening of your museum. In the first year, you might concentrate money and effort on the preparation of your physical facilities, so that a protective environment and adequate, well-equipped work space will be ready for your collections. In the second year, you might start meeting major objectives of your collecting or acquisitions plan and your research or documentation plan, along with attending to conservation as artifacts come in. Your interpretive program, including exhibits, might then get the major focus in the third year. Your fund raising, staff hiring, and training of volunteers could be phased accordingly.

But if your community is too impatient to let you prepare everything before going public, you may have to accelerate development, or at least open some temporary exhibits or start some programs for schools or outside groups at the same time that you carry out backstage preparations for a larger program, just to assure everyone that something really is happening at the new museum. That may mean planning to raise money and recruit personnel on a faster schedule than you'd intended. Either way, timing must be part of the plan.

Whatever you do, some individual needs to be put in overall charge of activities almost from the start. The earlier your museum's trustees or governing body designate a *director* of operations, the better. Ideally, the director will be in on the planning as well as taking day-to-day responsibility for carrying the plan out. At the latest, the engagement of a chief executive officer (called a *director* or *chief curator* in most museums) should come after the museum's purpose is adopted, the probability of community support is determined, an assessment is made of available collections and facilities, and the governing authority is established.

Museums have been developed and operated successfully by volunteer directors—at least, those volunteer directors who were willing and able to learn a lot of things quickly and make effective use of outside expertise, but *we recommend that you seek a director who already has formal training and experience in museum work, and that your director be paid.* It makes no more sense to turn over a community museum to an inexperienced volunteer to manage than it would to turn over the local high school or public library to an untrained person. In fact, the *salary* of your community's library director, school superintendent, or school principal is a reasonable guide to what your museum director should be paid, at least if your plans call for a museum of comparable budget size. Information on museum staff salaries is available from the American Association for State and Local History, the American Association of Museums, and from some regional and state museum associations. Even if you must begin without a paid, experienced museum director, you should plan for the support of truly professional staff eventually.

When you *can* seek a professional staff director, the advice that follows—on job advertisements, use of a search committee, and so on—is applicable to cities and counties creating museums, as well as to private organizations. Cities and counties should, of course, use their regular, established personnel procedures in seeking museum employees. In many instances, staff people in public museums will report to advisory boards, rather than to trustees, and ultimately the staff in a public museum is responsible to county commissioners, city managers, or another operating department.

Now: unless your museum's governing board itself is small, the board should designate no more than a half-dozen persons as a *search committee* to invite and evaluate applications for the position. Some museum boards engage professional "headhunters," firms that specialize in helping organizations find qualified employees, and they can be helpful, if you can afford them—particularly if your institution is large enough to warrant a far-reaching search for a real veteran of museum work. In any case, the board or search committee should write in plain English a realistic *description of the job* (see Appendix E) and of the qualifications considered necessary or desirable. Professionals in your state historical society, state museum, or state museum association can help you determine those things. Then you can advertise the position in the classified employment-opportunity sections of newspapers that have state or regional distribution and of periodicals published by museum associations, such as *Aviso* and *History News Dispatch*, the newsletters of the American Association of Museums and the American Association for State and Local History—publications in which museum professionals tend to look for job opportunities.

It's also a good idea to send copies of the job description and qualifications to directors of established museums and related cultural organizations in your state or region, with a request that they call the position to the attention of any professional they know who might be interested. But don't rely exclusively on word of mouth or "the old-boy network." For two things, failure to advertise openly denies you the opportunity to consider good candidates who otherwise won't get word about the position, and for another, it may put you in danger of violating equal-employment opportunity requirements.

Because subtle prejudices and even some overt discrimination lingers in our society, we'd like to emphasize that thoroughly well-qualified people trained in museum work include women as well as men, and both women and men from racial and ethnic minority groups.

You may wish to send your position description also to universities that have training programs in museum studies. These programs appear under varying titles—public history, historical administration, cultural-resource management, or something similar. Universities offering such courses often keep in touch with their graduates and provide job placement services. Lists of such university programs can be obtained from specialized museum associations, or from the Office of Museum Programs of the Smithsonian Institution in Washington, D.C., the American Association of Museums, and the American Association for State and Local History. Those organizations also can send you guidelines for such training programs to help you evaluate the adequacy of the training their graduates receive.

The job *advertisement* should include information on the salary range you can offer, fringe benefits, required or desirable qualifications, principal responsibilities, the closing date for submitting applications, the name of the contact person or group, the address to which applications should be sent, and assurances that the museum is an equal-opportunity or affirmative-action employer, open to candidates of either sex and any race. By mail, the search committee should respond to every applicant, acknowledging receipt of each application, and giving each applicant an idea of when to expect to hear further.

The search committee then should determine which applicants seem best for the job on paper and request references from those applicants—statements from previous employers or others who can comment knowledgeably on the experience and abilities of the applicants. Such information may be sought by mail or phone or both. Applicants whose references prove satisfactory should then be invited to come to your community for an interview, at the expense of the museum board, not the applicant. Before they come, you should provide them background information about the museum and the community or group it will serve, including the museum's governing document, mission statement, and any plans you may already have made. Ask each candidate to come separately, to meet with the search committee extensively and with other board members or the entire board at least casually, and to visit museum facilities and collections you already may have.

After completing the interviews, the search committee may want to ask the applicants for additional information or references. If, by then, no one candidate stands out, but more than one seems particularly impressive, the qualifying group may be invited for a second interview, this time with the entire board. In any event, the full board of the museum or other governing body should make the final decision after recommendations from the search committee. And when the board approves a candidate—preferably unanimously!—the board chairperson or president should negotiate with the successful candidate a *contract letter* specifying salary, fringe benefits, duties, limits of authority, length of appointment, standards or procedures for evaluation of performance, and procedures to follow if termination should be sought by either party. Given the current climate of ambiguity surrounding legal rights of employees, advance review of employment agreements by legal counsel for the museum is advisable. Rejected applicants should receive tactful letters as soon as possible after the decision is made.

Then, and only then, when an employment agreement has been reached with the board's choice, *public announcement* of the new director should be made. A press release to newspapers and radio and television stations in your area about the new director should be part of general publicity plans for the museum's development. And when the new director arrives, a welcoming reception can be helpful, to which—ideally—you would invite everyone in the community who is likely to be of help as the museum gets going. The new director will need to become a publicly recognizable representative of the new museum and will need the board's help to get acquainted in the community.

The museum-development plan you work out with the director will determine whether you'll need and can afford to hire *additional paid staff*, at full salary or part-time. No staff positions should be created without authorization from the board in long-range plans and annual budgets but once a position is authorized and budgeted, the staff director should have authority to fill it, not the board. That includes filling unpaid positions and engaging volunteers. A staff director cannot be held responsible for staff performance without having authority to select the rest of the staff.

Almost all museums, no matter how many paid professional staff members they have, also use *volunteers* to carry out valuable, sometimes essential, functions. Under proper supervision, volunteers can help with almost anything—driving busloads of school children to the museum, guiding tours through the museum's exhibits, taking tickets, helping with research, keeping records, or providing accounting services, legal counsel, and fund-raising leadership. Your plan should designate what parts of your programs can be carried out with the help of volunteers, so that provision can be made for recruiting and preparing them. Successful museums treat volunteers with as much care and respect as professional staff. Many museums have paid or volunteer *directors of volunteers*, who recruit and train these unpaid staff members and supervise their work.

It can be as useful to have job descriptions for volunteers as for paid staff. A word of caution: volunteers who merely "wander in off the street" should not automatically be accepted. *All* candidates for volunteer work need to be interviewed concerning experience, abilities, and interests, and each may legitimately be asked to provide references to check for such qualities as dependability and honesty. We recommend that, in accepting a volunteer, the museum put on paper in advance an agreement specifying what the volunteer will do, how many hours will be worked per week, and at what times of day or night that individual will be on the premises. Volunteers must be given work that is meaningful and satisfying to them as well as useful to the museum. Once they agree to do those things, however, they need to understand that the museum will depend on them. Volunteers who persistently come late or not at all, or who don't follow directions for their duties, or who interfere with paid staff on matters for which they are not qualified should be tactfully dismissed, just as paid staff should be dismissed in case of inadequate performance, unreliability, or insubordination.

Training for volunteers is essential and takes time and resources for which the long-range plan and annual budgets should provide. A retired school teacher may have great experience for conducting visitors through a historic-house museum three afternoons a week but that individual needs to be briefed on accurate information about the house, the length of the tour, ways to deal with special questions and problem situations, and the relationship of such volunteer work to the museum's mission and other activities overall. Moreover, tour guides or docents in particular should be monitored from time to time and evaluated. To be accepted, volunteers should agree, on joining the staff, to be routinely evaluated and to keep their work to high standards of performance. Treating volunteer work as the genuinely important element it is can enhance the satisfaction that good volunteers get from it—and the effort they put into it—and those who perform well should be rewarded with recognition by the board and professional staff.

Planning the use of human resources includes providing for their development. That is, as the museum develops, its paid and volunteer staff members will need *opportunities to improve* their skills and understanding. They can seek such opportunities through memberships in professional associations whose publications keep them abreast of the field—magazines, newsletters, technical reports, and books. Some associations also distribute audiovisual training programs and independent study courses that staff people can use in the museum where they work to learn new concepts and techniques or to improve their skills. Provision should be made as well to send professional staff and volunteers to occasional workshops and seminars in the museum field and to annual meetings of state, regional, and national associations that serve the field. Such meetings not only offer instructive formal presentations in their programs, but enable museum workers to get acquainted with their peers, share ideas with people dealing with similar problems, and learn where to get help when special needs arise throughout the year. Getting away to a professional meeting of one kind or another from time to time is a great way to recharge one's batteries, to keep up one's level of energy and enthusiasm. Your plan for staffing each of the museum's programs, then should not only involve numbers of people, volunteer and paid, but also clear definitions of the kinds and levels of expertise they will need and some plan for developing their abilities.

Those are the basic human-resource calculations needed for planning. Now comes the bottom line: What will the museum require in *financial resources*? What will each program, each part of the plan, including staffing, cost to carry out, over time?

Some expenses will be more or less fixed, necessary expenses for doing anything at all. *General overhead expenses* are in this category—such things as facility maintenance (heat, light, custodial, and security costs); basic personnel (at least the director's salary and fringe benefits); and care of collections, whether stored or on exhibit.

Other expenses will be *out-of-pocket*, incurred only if a particular special project is undertaken, such as construction costs of a new exhibit, transportation costs for a particular "outreach" activity, mailing costs of a special promotion, or printing costs for a new publication or brochure.

The plan needs to provide for reasonably dependable sources of funds for general, on-going operating expenses and to show what additional sources of funds the museum will try to tap for additional "out-of-pocket" expenditures.

Sooner or later, in the plan and in annual budgets, you'll need to estimate the costs of everything connected with the museum and calculate which *source of revenue* can realistically be expected to cover each cost. Will the county tax appropriations pay for staff salaries and fringe benefits? Will the city government provide utilities, maintenance, and security for the museum's building? Will membership dues or admission charges be necessary to cover other operating costs? Should certain special projects with heavy out-of-pocket costs be undertaken only if grants from corporations, foundations, or individuals are secured particularly for them? Will acquisitions each year depend on the success of an annual fund-raising event? Will interest from the endowment fund pay for research, conservation, or other things? Will additional fund raising be necessary to raise an endowment fund to provide interest income in each year's budget? Will a special capital-fund drive be needed for building renovation or expansion? And, if special fund raising is required, who will do it? When? And how will fund raising itself be financed? The plan is not complete until you identify realistic sources of funds for all on-going activities and special programs and budget for fund raising itself.

In this kind of planning, it is useful to visit other museums to learn what different kinds of functions cost *them*, and to use outside museum consultants if you have no professional director yet. Business executives on your board also may have experience that they can be asked to contribute in estimating costs, evaluating alternative sources of supplies, judging the cost-effectiveness of operations and proposals, and maintaining financial controls. Your goal, of course, is not that of a business—to make a financial profit; rather, you are trying to produce a *cultural payoff* for your community on its investment in the museum. Nonetheless, the museum is like a business in being unable to operate very long at a financial loss. Unless some wealthy individual is willing to underwrite your losses every year, *financial planning* will be as necessary for your museum as for the local car dealership or General Motors.

Studies have indicated that aggressive leaders in the business world typically take a passive approach to service on nonprofit boards of directors. If you can entice them to help, however, their skills and experience in assessing risks, weighing alternative investment options, controlling costs, and developing plans on a sound financial footing are as needed in organizations that yield cultural dividends as they are in organizations that yield dollar profits. Moreover, once a financial plan to provide the necessary resources for a museum is agreed upon by a board, all board members have responsibility to see that the necessary funding is secured. That may mean soliciting private contributions, lobbying for government funds, calling on corporations and foundations, and giving generously oneself. No responsible staff overspends its budget and then blithely expects the board to make up the difference. Similarly, no responsible board approves a financial plan and budget and then leaves it to staff people to find the money. And no museum lasts long without planning in detail how it will finance its operations.

So these four questions are added to your basic checklist for planning:

13. What time schedule for development will the museum follow?

14. What staff, paid and volunteer, will be needed?

15. What will each part of the plan cost to carry out?

16. Where will the money come from?

For more information

On providing the human resources museums need, we recommend these publications:

The Wages of History: The AASLH Employment Trends and Salary Survey (87 pages), by Charles Phillips and Patricia Hogan. Nashville: AASLH, 1985.

"How to Hire a Director," by Bryant F. Tolles, Jr., *History News* 40 (March 1985).

The Effective Management of Volunteer Programs (197 pages), by Marlene Wilson. Volunteer Management Associates, 1976. The address for Volunteer Management Associates is 279 South Cedar Brook Road, Boulder, Colorado 80302.

Survival Skills for Managers (264 pages), by Marlene Wilson.

264 pages, Boulder, Colorado: Volunteer Mangement Associates, 1981.

Management Principles for Non-Profit Agencies and Organizations (584 pages), edited by Gerald Zaltman. New York: American Management Association, 1979.

On providing financial resources that museums need, we recommend the following:

Securing Grant Support: Effective Planning and Preparation, by William T. Alderson, AASLH Technical Leaflet 62, AASLH, Nashville, Tennessee.

The Art of Asking: How to Solicit Philanthropic Gifts (176 pages), by Paul H. Schneiter. Ambler, Pa.: Fund-Raising Institute, 1985.

The Complete Guide to Corporate Fund Raising (112 pages), by Joseph Dermer and Stephen Westheimer. Hartsdale, N.Y.: Public Service Materials Center, 1982.

Enterprise in the Nonprofit Sector (141 pages), by James C. Crimmins and Mary Keil. Washington, D.C., and New York: Partners for Livable Places and the Rockefeller Brothers Fund, 1983.

10

Now Will It Really Work?

CONGRATULATIONS! You now have the rudiments of a museum development plan. And when you've carried it out, there you'll be with a wonderful museum, right? Well, let's speed up the reel just a few feet ahead, to the place where we've come to visit your museum, now that it's operational.

As chairperson of the board of trustees, you pick us up at the airport and get us to the museum in time for the board's big meeting, just after the end of the fiscal year. There the carefully kept minutes of the last meeting are read by the secretary and approved. The treasurer reports that income for the year has covered expenses and that fund-raising goals have been met from all anticipated sources. The chair of the acquisitions committee reports that artifacts have been acquired on schedule, so far, to fill in gaps in the collections. The director reports that all key staff positions are filled and that all activities are on schedule; that the reference library is established and documentation has been completed for items to be used in the first permanent and temporary exhibits, which are ready to open; that unexhibited objects are in storage areas that meet acceptable standards for conservation, and that publications, school programs, and other interpretive activities are proceeding on a coordinated basis. The director of volunteers announces that volunteers have been trained to conduct tours and help with research. The volunteer lawyer on the board reports that all documents are in order, including tax-exempt certification, the collections policy, and letters of agreement with staff and volunteers. The chair of the membership committee reports that the initial membership goal has been reached. Everything appears to be covered, and all is well. Right?

Sorry. There are still some important things missing from your meeting, most of which come under the heading of *reality*.

In Heaven, perhaps, a plan may provide a perfect blueprint for what actually happens; but on earth, the best-made plans of mice and museums inevitably go astray. Your museum will work well only if some other people are present at this mythical meeting—people whose participation will help you adjust to inevitable imperfections.

For example, there should also be a *report from an independent auditor*, a certified public accountant, whom you hire (if a CPA firm won't volunteer its services) to determine whether, in fact, the treasurer's report and the museum's financial statements are free of errors. The audit firm will prepare an objective, written opinion on whether your financial statements present fairly the financial position of your organization—the assets and liabilities on its balance sheet, the income and expenses on its activity statement (in business, called the *profit and loss statement*). The auditors may submit other financial statements, such as a report on your uses of cash—all, to use the auditors' language, "in accordance with generally accepted accounting principles."

In the real world, you are also likely to have a report from the secretary of the board on *amendments* that have been proposed to the bylaws or even to the constitution of the museum. Such documents need periodic review and at least occasionally are going to require changing provisions that haven't worked very well or don't adequately cover questions that have arisen. Records of such changes need to be kept carefully and reported to the Internal Revenue Service, to protect your tax-exempt status.

Also, in the real world, you'll need a report from the chairperson of the publicity committee, explaining what the committee has done, and with what success, to arouse public interest in using the museum—because it's quite possible to develop a wonderful museum entirely according to plan, only to discover one flaw: Nobody comes. That will happen if nobody tells the public about it.

Indeed, at the meeting we are attending with you, is there anybody present from outside the museum? This is the annual meeting of an institution that purports to be of public benefit and may even be using public funds. Where is the local press? If nothing on your agenda is so sensitive that your legal counsel advises going into executive session to deal with it, you'll want the press there, to help keep the public informed of the way in which you are handling its money and of the things you are trying to provide. Also, where are representatives of groups outside the museum who work with or have interest in it? Where are teachers who have been working with your museum on school programs? Where are representatives of other counties or communities with which you are working to provide traveling exhibits? Where are major contributors of collections or funds who deserve to be publicly recognized? Where are politicians who have been sympathetic to your cause?

Not all such people should necessarily be invited to routine board meetings, but the museum is incomplete without keeping them, one way or another, informed and involved with the museum's activities. If such people begin to feel ignored, left out, or unrewarded, you'll certainly eventually have visitors at your meetings—angry ones who may not have been expected, let alone invited. Political or public relations "fence maintenance" is a continuing museum requirement.

Moreover, what means have you, yourself, set up to *evaluate* the museum's programs, now that they're in place? Suppose that school kids don't actually learn what you thought your guides and special school materials were so wonderfully ready to teach them? What if the adult public mostly stands around in front of your carefully prepared exhibits and yawns? It's helpful to keep track of the numbers of people who visit your museum, but that doesn't say much about the quality of the experience they undergo there. Have you planned to do any checking with questionnaires or interviews with visitors to see what in the museum's programs has been most meaningful to them and what was not?

Evaluation is difficult to do, and we don't recommend that you make every visitor stop at the exit door and take a test; but unless you solicit some kind of feedback, you can't rest assured that you are meeting your public-benefit goals, and you won't know what needs improvement in the future. Nor can you prove to potential donors or grant-makers that you are effective, on the one hand, or, on the other, that you genuinely need help to make improvements.

Alas, that's still not all. In the real world there still must be a report from the *planning* committee. That is because your plan needs regular review and revision, in light of things you didn't know would happen. Plans need to be adjusted to accommodate opportunities and obstacles that you didn't foresee, as well as successes and disappointments. If your fund-raising drive nets twice what you estimated, obviously you can afford to expand or accelerate your previous plans. Conversely, you'll be forced to reduce them if the fund-raising drive falls short. Also, you have to adjust for what you can't control—inflationary hikes in your operating costs, for example. And obviously you can't proceed on your plan's original assumptions if a major acquisition turns out to cost much more than you thought, or if a major financial supporter backs out, or if a donor withdraws a collection offer, or a tornado rips off your roof.

A plan is a guideline for reaching objectives based on *reasonable guesses* in the present about the future. Plans should be reviewed at least annually, preferably quarterly, and in some instances even monthly, to see whether objectives are being met on schedule and if not, why not. Financial reports, of course, should be produced and reviewed every month. Moreover, planning needs to be extended regularly. Each year the long-range plan should be added to by at least one additional year, so that there always exists a long-range plan. Thus planning is a regular, ongoing museum function, not a one-time, up-front activity.

All right; now—at last—we have a well-developed museum organization capable of coping with change and the rest of the world. So—now, at your meeting, the auditor warrants that the financial statements are reliable, but some of your financial controls need a little tightening. The board's secretary recommends some bylaw changes to make one of the governing procedures less cumbersome and the nominating procedures more fair. Reporters take notes and ask questions, so that they can report on the museum's doings to the entire community, whose interest the publicity committee is not taking for granted. The board will discuss the significance of information presented by the director from a spot survey of museum visitors about their reactions to the newest exhibit. And a teacher from an adjoining county will give the board a fresh perspective on what is needed and expected from the museum by the schools there. Also, the director or the planning-committee chairperson will propose changes in the long-range plan that will enable the museum to maintain its mission and meet its basic goals, yet cope with significant change.

At the end of that kind of meeting, we will be ready to congratulate you. Yes, you now have an impressive museum. And you have done it by answering these final four questions on your basic ckecklist for planning:

17. How will you maintain good public relations?
18. How will you provide for continual planning?
19. How will you evaluate your museum's activities?
20. How will you keep your museum alive, dynamic, creative, and visionary?

Let us conclude with a parting word about that last question.

There used to be a colorful advertisement for museums—a big poster—in the London underground, with this message on it: "Local museums are treasure houses where unlikely objects—curious, ingenious, comic, even beautiful—lie stranded for our gaze. They indicate local pride and a sense of identity. More vividly evocative of the everyday past than our grander institutions, they deserve and reward our notice."

Stranded is hardly the right word, particularly if you put into a museum all the care that we have outlined in this book; but how true the rest of the description can be! And how useful to remember, after so many technical considerations, that the intent of it all is truly to produce a *treasure house.* Caring for the things we humans treasure and explaining why we treasure them is the essential mission of museums, whether we pursue it through scientific description, intellectual education, or aesthetic appreciation. Let's remember also that we don't always know why an ancient spearpoint, a face in an old photograph, the bones of some extinct animal, or a particular painting so captures our imagination and remains meaningful in our lives long after we leave a museum. *We know only that all the effort it takes to make a good museum is worthwhile if and when a museum experience gives someone pleasure, arouses emotions, or stimulates thought.* Please plan to keep that in mind, too!

So—there you have it. We've done our best to help you learn the basics. Thanks for your decision to take museum work seriously. Good luck and best wishes!

For more information

On topics covered in this chapter, we recommend these publications:

Museum Public Relations, AASLH Museum Management Series Vol. 2 (237 pages), by G. Donald Adams. Nashville: American Association for State and Local History, 1983.

Museum Accounting Handbook (158 pages), by William H. Daughtrey, Jr., and Malvern J. Gross, Jr. Washington, D.C.: American Association of Museums, 1978.

Marketing for Non-Profit Organizations (436 pages), by Philip Kotler. Englewood Cliffs, N.J.: Prentice-Hall, 1975.

"Exhibit Evaluation—A Goal Referenced Approach," by Chandler G. Screven, in *Curator* 19 (1976): 271-290.

A Preliminary Guide for Conducting Naturalistic Evaluation in Studying Museum Environments, by Robert L. Wolf and Barbara L. Tymitz. Washington, D.C.: Office of Museum Programs, Smithsonian Institution, 1978.

For all museum topics, the following bibliographies will provide more helpful references:

A Museum Management Bibliography, by Louis F. Gorr. American Association of Museums, *Museum News* Reprints (May-June 1980): 71-84; (July-August 1980):67-77.

An Annotated Bibliography for the Development and Operation of Historic Sites, by the AAM Historic Sites Committee. Washington, D.C.: American Association of Museum, 1982.

A Bibliography on Historical Organization Practices, edited by Federick L. Rath, Jr., and Merrilyn Rogers O'Connell, 6 vols. Nashville: American Association for State and Local History, 1975-1983. Series covers administration, documentation, interpretation, conservation, historic preservation, and research.

Part III

Some Basic Documents

A

Sample Museum Bylaws

THE BYLAWS presented here are not meant as a model for every museum. Each museum is different, and bylaws must vary to reflect particular museum situations. This example is merely a starting point for a museum planning group to use in considering what kind of organization it wishes to develop and what kind of legal document might be generated to express that wish.

ANYTOWN MUSEUM AND ART CENTER BYLAWS

Article I

Organization and Location

Section 1.0. The Anytown Museum and Art Center is a _____ nonprofit Corporation with its principal office in the City of_____ in_____ County, _____.

Article II

Purpose

Section 2.0. The Corporation's purposes are as set forth in its Articles of Incorporation, which were approved by the Secretary of the State of _____ on _____ (date). The general purpose shall be to promote, through the establishment and maintenance of a museum and allied projects, a program that will bring about a better understanding and appreciation by the community of its history, art, and natural environment.

Article III

Management

Section 3.0. The management of this Corporation shall be vested in a Board of Trustees (hereinafter sometimes called the "Board") consisting of not more than (_____) members to be elected as prescribed in Section 3.1.

Section 3.1. The terms of one-third (1/3) of the Members of the Board shall expire at each Annual Meeting; their successors shall be elected at the Board's preceding regular January quarterly meeting, to take office at the next Annual Meeting. A Member's regular term shall be three (3) years, or until a successor is duly qualified; no member shall be elected to more than two (2) successive full terms; however, an immediate Past President may be elected for an additional successive one-year (1) term if not then a member of the Board.

Section 3.2. The Board shall choose the remainder of its new Members; the candidates therefore shall be recommended by the nominating committee in consultation with the Executive Committee and the Director, who shall give consideration to broad representation of various community interests and organizations.

Section 3.3. Any Member of the Board who shall be absent from three meetings a year without presenting satisfactory excuses shall be deemed to have resigned from the Board and shall cease to be a Member thereof, subject to reinstatement by majority vote of the Board. In the event of such vacancy, or in the event of any vacancy on the Board, it may elect a successor at any duly convened meeting.

Section 3.4. The Annual Meeting of the Board shall be held on the first Tuesday in April of each year. The Board shall have quarterly meetings on the first Tuesdays of January, April, July, and October. Special meetings shall be called by the Secretary upon written request of seven (7) Members of the Board; written notice thereof shall be mailed to all Members of the Board at least five (5) days prior to the day set for such meetings. Written notice of the Annual Meeting shall be mailed to all Members of the Board at least ten (10) days prior to the day set for such meeting. The Secretary shall serve, or attend to the serving of, all notices.

Section 3.5. The meetings of the Board and all its Committees shall be conducted according to the latest revision of *Robert's Rules of Order,* but it shall be necessary in any event for a quorum to be present for the Board or any of its committees to act. A quorum for any such meeting shall be a majority of those entitled to notice of such meetings.

Section 3.6. The Board shall assume the management of the Corporation. It shall receive and act upon all committee reports, those of its Officers and of the Director. It shall determine the policies of the administration and operation of the Museum and Art Center; it shall assume responsibility for the finances and responsibility for the ethical standards of the Museum and Art Center.

Section 3.7. The Board shall have an Executive Committee which shall act for the Board between meetings thereof. The Executive Committee shall be composed of seven (7) members who shall be the officers, the immediate Past President, and one (1) member-at-large.

Section 3.8. The Board may from time to time appoint ex-officio members as it desires. All ex-officio appointments shall terminate at the following Annual Meeting of the Board, and no ex-officio members shall be entitled to vote or be counted for quorum purposes.

Article IV
Officers
Section 4.0. The Officers of the Corporation shall be elected President, First Vice-President, and Second Vice-President, a Secretary, and a Treasurer, each of whom shall be elected for a term of one (1) year or until a successor is duly qualified.

Section 4.1. No officer shall be eligible for re-election after serving two (2) terms in office until at least one (1) year shall have expired after his or her last term of office.

Section 4.2. At least sixty (60) days prior to the Board's regular quarterly January Meeting, the President shall appoint a nominating committee consisting of five (5) Members of the Board. This committee shall investigate the qualification and availability of persons who might serve as Officers, and shall report its recommendations for such positions by letter to the Board at least thirty (30) days prior to its January Meeting.

Section 4.3. Additional nominations may be made by any Member of the Board with the consent of the nominee. The Officers shall be elected by majority vote of the Board at its regular January quarterly Meeting, and the Officers so elected shall take office at the following Annual Meeting.

Section 4.4. The duties of the Officers shall be as follows:

Section 4.41. President: The President shall preside at all meetings of the Board and its Executive Committee. He or she shall appoint all committees and shall be ex-officio a member of each committee. He or she shall also perform all the usual functions of the President of a _____ nonprofit Corporation.

Section 4.42. First Vice-President: In the event of the absence of the President or the President's inability or refusal to carry out such duties, the First Vice-President shall assume such duties. He or she shall chair one of the standing committees.

Section 4.43. Second Vice-President: In the event of the absence of the First Vice-President or his or her inability or refusal to perform such duties, the Second Vice-President shall assume such duties. He or she shall chair one of the standing committees.

Section 4.44. Treasurer: The Treasurer, with assistance from the Director, shall keep an accurate record of all monies received and disbursed by the Corporation; such records shall be kept on file at a place designated by the Executive Committee. He or she shall deposit all monies received in one or more banks and/or savings and loan institutions located in the City of _____, to the credit of the Corporation, and he or she shall make investments in such assets as are approved by the Board. All of such investments shall be in the name of the Corporation. Upon the approval of the Board or its Executive Committee, the Treasurer shall use the available funds of the Corporation to pay all of its just bills. At each Annual Meeting, the Treasurer shall submit a written report for the fiscal year just ended.

Section 4.45. Vacancies: A vacancy in any office due to any cause whatsoever shall be filled for the remainder of its current term by the Board of Trustees at a duly convened meeting if the notice thereof contains advice of such election.

Article V
Museum and Art Center Director

Section 5.0 The Board of Trustees may appoint a Director, who shall be in charge of the operation of the Museum and Art Center. The Director shall be responsible for its administration and its activities, according to the policies established by the Board. He or she shall have authority to employ and dismiss personnel of the staff in accordance with policies and budgets approved by the Board. The Director shall submit an Annual Report at the Annual Meeting on the conditions and activities of the Museum and Art Center, and he or she shall make such recommendations in regard thereto as he or she sees fit. The Director shall submit informal progress reports at the meetings of the Board and its Executive Committee, and he or she shall call to their attention any matters requiring action or notice.

Article VI
Committees

Section 6.0. The Board may by resolution designate one (1) or more committees; each committee shall have and may exercise powers as provided by the Board. Such committee or committees shall have such name or names as the Board may determine.

Section 6.1. The committees shall keep regular minutes of their proceedings and report the same to the Board when required.

Section 6.2. The Board's standing committees may include: Acquisitions, Activities and Programs, Building and Grounds, Exhibits, Finance and Budget, Membership, Memorials, Personnel, Public Relations, and Standing Rules, or others as needed.

Section 6.3. The chairs of the standing committees shall be members of the Board. Standing committees shall consist of two (2) members of the Board and others deemed qualified by the President.

Section 6.4. The membership of all other committees shall be in such number and for such terms as the President shall designate.

Article VII
Advisory Board
Section 7.0. Members of an Advisory Board may be nominated by the Executive Committee and elected by the Board at its Annual Meeting. A prerequisite to such membership shall be the ability and insight to make a specific contribution to the Museum and Art Center and its activities. Re-election to the Advisory Board shall be only after service on one of the Advisory Board's committees or after specific contributions in support of the Corporation's activities and purposes. Such membership shall be without the privilege of voting on the policies or management of the Corporation, and no member of the Advisory Board shall be counted for quorum purposes.

Section 7.1. Members of the Advisory Board shall attend the Annual Meeting held on the first Tuesday in April. A regular meeting of the Advisory Board shall be held on the second Tuesday in October of each year.

Article VIII
Financial Matters
Section 8.0. No funds of the Corporation shall be invested or expended without authorization of the Board.

Section 8.1. The Board shall designate the Corporation's fiscal year. The books of account of the Corporation shall be balanced and audited by a Certified Public Accountant at the close of the fiscal year.

Section 8.2. The Director, and other employees as determined by the Board, from time to time shall be bonded in amounts, for the purposes and with the corporate sureties acceptable to the Board.

Article IX
Amendments
Section 9.0. Alterations, amendments, or repeals of these Bylaws may

be made by a majority of the Members of the Board entitled to vote at any Annual or Quarterly Meeting if the notice thereof contains a statement of the proposed alteration, amendment, or repeal.

Article X
Annual Reports
Section 10.0. Each officer and those committee chairpersons so designated by the Board shall render annual written reports of the activities of their respective offices or committees. Such reports shall be filed with the Secretary at the Annual Meeting. An Annual Report of the Anytown Museum and Art Center shall be published immediately after the Annual Meeting.

Article XI
Dissolution
Section 11.0. Should the museum at any time permanently cease to function as a museum, the buildings and real property shall remain in place and be turned over to the _____ County Court to be used at its discretion for other educational purposes.

Section 11.1. Artifacts and personalty that are the permanent property of the museum shall be transferred to another museum or educational institution within the area. Should there be outstanding debts owed by the museum, sufficient of said personalty may be sold to satisfy creditors.

Section 11.2. Personal artifacts on loan to the museum must be returned to the donors as authorized by the signatures of the _____ County Judge and the President of the Board of Trustees.

Section 11.3. After the Corporation permanently abandons the operation of the museum, the endowment fund as created and described shall revert in full to _____ County to be used by any one or more educational institutions with _____ County, _____, such institutions to be named by the County Commissioners Court.

_____ County, _____, subject to applicable state laws.

B

Standard Accession Record

ANYTOWN MUSEUM AND ART CENTER

_____Gift

_____Purchase $_____

_____Exchange

_____Field Collection

_____Loan

Accession No. _____ Received by _____

Date of accession _____

Object name _____

Materials _____

Maker/artist/manufacturer _____

Place of origin _____

Description _____

_____

_____

_____

Condition _____

_____

_____

Value _____

Dimensions _____

Name, address, and telephone number of immediate source:

_____

_____

_____

Dates of ownership _____

Previous owner _____ Dates _____

Previous owner _____ Dates _____

Documents accompanying acquisition _____

_____

Donor information (use, age, association with places, individuals or events) _____

_____

_____

Location _____ Date _____

Accepted by _____ * Accessioned by _____

Catalogued by _____

Bibliographical, photographic, documentary cross-references

_____

_____

_____

Restrictions _____

Remarks _____

_____

*Include reference to page of minutes of Board action.

C

Typical Museum Budget List

EACH MUSEUM is unique, so the budget process will vary, according to the type of museum and programs provided by the museum. Therefore, the following basic budget list should not be considered as all-inclusive. Carefully consider all sources of potential income for your museum and all expenses for the programs you plan for the next year.

INCOME
Contributions
Membership Dues
Admissions
Museum Store Sales
Special Events
Program Income
Interest from Investments

EXPENSES
Salaries
Payroll Taxes
Fringe Benefits
Conservation
Utilities
Maintenance
Office Supplies
Supplies for Educational Program

Exhibit Expense
Insurance
Museum Store Expense
Publications (PR, brochures, etc.)
Vehicles (maintenance, gas, and oil)
Cleaning Supplies
Consultant Fees
Professional Memberships and Subscriptions
Staff Travel

Remember to budget all up-front expenses for any special event, museum store stock, and programs or publications from which you expect income later. More details on budgeting may be found in the *Museum Accounting Handbook* published by the American Association of Museums, Chapter 10, page 93.

D

Recommended Certificate of Gift

CERTIFICATE OF GIFT

Name of Donor _____

Address _____

Description of Gift:

I (we), being the sole legal owner(s) of the property described above, hereby give the the Anytime Museum and Art Center, for its use and benefit without restriction as to use or disposition, the property described above. In addition, I (we) give all copyright and associated rights I (we) have. To the best of my (our) knowledge I (we) have good and complete right, title, and interest (including all transferred copyright, trademark, and related interests) to give. I (we) have no objections to my (our) name(s) appearing as donor(s) in connection with this gift in Museum records, publications, and other descriptions.

_____ Date
_____ Signature
_____ Signature

E

Sample Job Description

Job Title: Director

Classification: (if part of a government organization)

Education: Bachelor's degree minimum and advanced degree preferred in museum studies or a discipline related to the museum's mission and collections.

Experience, skills and knowledge: Organizational and administrative ability. Ability to initiate programs, train and motivate people, coordinate activities, speak publicly, and deal effectively with the public, private groups and community organizations. Considerable knowledge of and interest in the subject matter dealt with by the museum. Should understand museum development and be able to communicate that understanding to the Board and others outside the museum field. Minimum of five years' experience in museum work. Previous managerial or supervisory experience preferred.

Job Description: 1. Responsible for orientation, training, work assignments, motivation, and evaluation of other staff and volunteers.

2. Responsible for development of plans and

139

budgets for consideration by the Board and for implementation of approved plans and budgets.

3. Responsible for establishing and maintaining appropriate records, forms, procedures and practices relating to collections, personnel, purchasing and general administration.

4. Responsible for building security, visitor safety, and maintenance of facilities and equipment.

5. Responsible for developing and carrying out all on-going activities and special programs of the museum with budgets and policies authorized by the Board.

6. Attends all meetings of the Board and its committees, maintains liaison with them, provides financial and other reports as requested by the Board, and maintains public relations broadly in the community.

Compensation: Includes salary, medical insurance, retirement-plan contribution, sick leave, vacation time, and paid opportunities for professional development such as attendance at annual meetings of relevant professional associations.

F

Basic Organization Chart

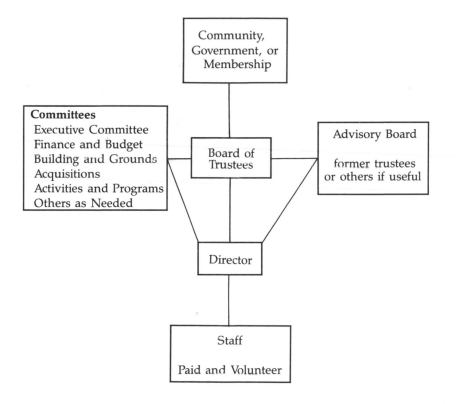

Index

142